CULTURE SMART!

HUNGARY

Brian McLean and Kester Eddy

·K·U·P·E·R·A·R·D·

This book is available for special discounts for bulk purchases for sales promotions or premiums. Special editions, including personalized covers, excerpts of existing books, and corporate imprints, can be created in large quantities for special needs.

For more information contact Kuperard publishers at the address below.

ISBN 978 1 85733 868 3

British Library Cataloguing in Publication Data
A CIP catalogue entry for this book is available from the British Library

First published in Great Britain
by Kuperard, an imprint of Bravo Ltd
59 Hutton Grove, London N12 8DS
Tel: +44 (0) 20 8446 2440   Fax: +44 (0) 20 8446 2441
www.culturesmart.co.uk
Inquiries: sales@kuperard.co.uk

Series Editor Geoffrey Chesler
Design Bobby Birchall

Printed in Malaysia

About the Author

BRIAN McLEAN is a British translator and journalist who, after periods in Japan and Austria, settled in Hungary in 1977. He is the author of *Escape Routes: Ten Excursions from Budapest*. He has translated about fifty, mainly scholarly, books, including Gabriella Balla's *Herend* (an illustrated history of the porcelain factory), *Political Economy of Socialism* by János Kornai, and *The Holy Crown of Hungary* by Endre Tóth and Károly Szelényi.

KESTER EDDY is a British journalist, primarily in print, but with stints on radio and television. He traveled widely in Europe, Asia, and Southern Africa as a photographic journalist before settling in Budapest in 1986, from where he has reported on Hungary and the region for outlets such as the *Financial Times*, *Economist Intelligence Unit*, and *Business New Europe-Intellinews*.

The Culture Smart! series is continuing to expand. All Culture Smart! guides are available as e-books, and many as audio books. For latest titles visit

www.culturesmart.co.uk

The publishers would like to thank **CultureSmart!**Consulting for its help in researching and developing the concept for this series.

CultureSmart!Consulting creates tailor-made seminars and consultancy programs to meet a wide range of corporate, public-sector, and individual needs. Whether delivering courses on multicultural team building in the USA, preparing Chinese engineers for a posting in Europe, training call-center staff in India, or raising the awareness of police forces to the needs of diverse ethnic communities, it provides essential, practical, and powerful skills worldwide to an increasingly international workforce.

For details, visit www.culturesmartconsulting.com

CultureSmart!Consulting and **CultureSmart!** guides have both contributed to and featured regularly in the weekly travel program "Fast Track" on BBC World TV.

contents

contents

Map of Hungary

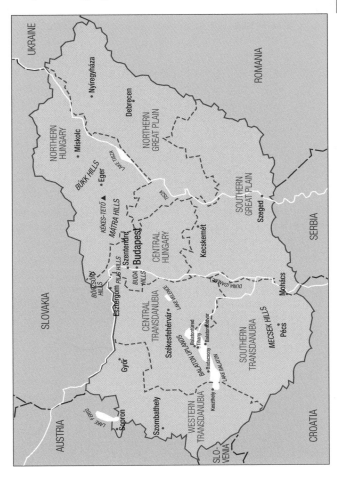

introduction

Hungary's reputation for hospitality dates back a thousand years. St. Stephen, the country's first king, wrote in the early eleventh century, "Visitors and newcomers bring such gain that they may worthily stand in sixth place in royal dignity."

But the TV images in 2015 of Hungarian soldiers building a border fence to keep out war-scarred Syrian refugees has sullied that reputation—even as local volunteers stood by in the heat handing out drink and food within sight of the barrier being erected.

In truth, Hungarians' views of themselves is in a high state of flux, challenged by the fast-moving dynamics of the modern world. Individually, the Hungarian belief in the importance of learning from abroad has changed little, and this combination of good-natured openness and self-respect is a very attractive trait. Yet collectively, a combination of factors—including long-standing fear of change, of losing identity, of general insecurity—at times make Magyars appear aloof, arrogant, even truculent.

Expatriate managers and foreign diplomats speak about the warmth and welcome they have felt in Hungary. And, for the most part, it is genuine. Yet, as one departing West European ambassador confided in private: "You can't teach them anything, can you?"

All this is worth emphasizing especially because of Hungary's recent history. From the end of the Second World War until 1990, Hungary was part of the Soviet bloc, that Eastern Europe of workers, tractors, factories, drab clothes, and dull streets. Today, Hungarians feel part of Central Europe once again, the Europe of the Habsburg empire, full of Baroque churches and sturdy nineteenth-century architecture.

In a religious and intellectual sense, Hungary lies north and west of the dividing line between Catholic/ Protestant Europe and Eastern Orthodox Europe. Now there's another division running through Hungarian society. It's like the old divide in France between Catholic and anticlerical. The two strands were known here in the 1930s as *nép-nemzeti* and *urbánus*, which today translate into "conservative" and "liberal." Many are dismayed to see this division back—and so starkly—but it's best to be aware of it. Churchgoing, choosing a school, seeing a film or play, even going to a restaurant, can be political act.

So what are modern Hungarians like? Paradoxical, you could say. They are talkative, but reticent; they are voluble, amusing, and full of an irony verging on cynicism. But beneath the self-denigration lies a strong confidence in their own culture, way of life, and achievements against all the historical odds. This faith in themselves is a private matter that they may not like to bother you with. (Or they may insist you know all about it!) They love to solve problems and overcome a crisis, but they may lose interest when everything's running smoothly. They are cheerful, but doleful. There's fatalism mixed into the optimism, and resentment found among the pride. There's no easy way to sum up the fascinating complexity of the Hungarian character. Knowledge, the key to understanding, is what *Culture Smart! Hungary* sets out to provide. Read on, and enjoy the journey!

Key Facts

Official Name	Hungary/ *Magyarország* (since 2012)	Hungary joined the EU on May 1, 2004.
Capital City	Budapest. Pop. 1.7 million	Buda, Pest, and Óbuda merged in 1876.
Other Main Cities	Debrecen, Miskolc, Szeged, Pécs, Győr	
Area	35,919 sq. miles (93,030 sq. km)	
Climate	Temperate, with changeable weather. Drier and more extreme from W to E.	
Population	9,830,000 (Jan. 2016)	Density: 274 per sq. mile (106 per sq. km)
Ethnic Makeup	Almost all see themselves as Hungarian, some also as Roma (Gypsy, 7.5%), German (2.1%), or Slovak (1%), etc. Some 1.5 percent of population are foreign nationals.	
Language	Hungarian (Magyar) is the official language and first language of 98.5%.	English and German are the main foreign languages taught in schools.
Religion	37% of Hungarians are Roman Catholic, 11.5% Calvinist, 2.2% Evangelical (Lutheran), 1.8% Greek Catholic, and 0.1% religious Jews (2011 census). All "historical churches" receive state support.	
Government	Parliamentary democracy. Single-chamber parliament of 199 MPs, 106 elected by constituency and 93 by party list. Head of state is the president. Head of government is the prime minister.	Local government, mayors, and European MPs elected by residents. The 7 EU regions cover 19 counties, Budapest, and 22 cities with county status.

Currency	Hungarian forint	Paper: 500, 1000, 2000, 5000, 10,000, 20,000 Coins: 200–5
Hungarians Abroad	Some 5 million Hungarians live abroad (3 million in neighboring countries, within pre-First World War "historical" Hungary).	Large Hungarian communities exist in the USA, Germany, Canada, etc., but rapid assimilation makes them hard to quantify.
Media	6 state TV and 7 state radio stations nationwide; 2 national commercial TV networks; 4 main national dailies, 1 free daily, 1 financial daily, several tabloids, 19 provincial dailies.	Budapest has 1 English- and 1 German-lang. weekly, plus 1 fortnightly business paper. State news agency MTI and others provide wire, Internet, and newsletter services in English.
Electricity	230 volts, 50 Hz	Standard European plugs and sockets. UK appliances need adapters, US/Canadian transformers too.
TV, Video, and DVD	PAL B system	Not compatible with US videos
Internet Domain	.hu	
Telephone	Hungary's country code is 36.	To dial out, dial 00 for international, 06 for domestic trunk and mobile calls.
Time Zone	CET (Central European Time), GMT + 1 hour	Daylight saving in summer – forward 1 hour

chapter one

LAND & PEOPLE

"Hazám, hazám . . . "

"Homeland, my homeland, my all! My whole life I owe to thee," sings the troubled medieval patriot Bánk bán in the eponymous 1860 opera by the Hungarian composer Ferenc Erkel. You won't meet a Hungarian who disagrees. People from larger countries may sometimes take theirs for granted, but not people from smaller, more vulnerable countries like Hungary. Patriotism there runs as deep as deep can be.

GEOGRAPHICAL MATTERS

Hungary is a landlocked country in the center of Europe. Budapest, the capital, lies about 890 miles (1,425 km) from London, 980 miles (1,575 km) from Moscow, 500 miles (800 km) from Rome, and 655 miles (1,050 km) from Istanbul, as the crow flies. Hungary's area of 35,919 square miles (93,032 sq. km) makes it similar in size to Portugal, or to the state of Indiana. It has an irregular egg shape.

Hungary occupies the center of the large, relatively flat Carpathian Basin. It is surrounded by the Alps, the Carpathians, and the Dinaric Alps, but none of these ranges extend into Hungary, where the highest point—the peak of Kékes-tető, 60 miles (95 km) east of

Budapest—is only 3,326 feet (1,014 m) above sea level. Going clockwise, the countries across Hungary's 1,377 miles (2,217 km) of frontier are Austria, Slovakia, Ukraine, Romania, Serbia, Croatia, and Slovenia.

The Danube, Europe's second-longest river after the Volga, arrives from Slovakia and follows the border east, before turning due south to bisect the country and enter Serbia. The part of Hungary to the west of it is called Transdanubia (Dunántúl). To the east lie the Northern Uplands (Északi hegység) and the Great Plain (Alföld).

Transdanubia has three major lakes, all shallow and fringed with reeds. The largest by far is Balaton (232 square miles, or 600 sq. km). The second is Fertő (Neusiedlersee), straddling the border with Austria. Between Balaton and Budapest lies Lake Velence.

The main ranges of hills in Hungary form an almost straight line from southwest to northeast, from the Balaton Uplands to Buda Hills and continuing on the opposite side of the Danube as the Northern Uplands. The western border with Austria runs through Alpine foothills.

Badacsony, overlooking Lake Balaton, is one of several obvious extinct volcanoes in Hungary, but there are no active ones today. No earthquake recorded in the territory of present-day Hungary has had a magnitude greater than 6 on the Richter scale. The last earthquake fatality was in 1956 at Dunaharaszti, south of Budapest, when a makeshift house collapsed.

The population of Hungary peaked at around 10.7 million in 1981 (similar to that of Ohio or Illinois), but has since fallen to 9.8 million (January, 2016). The population density of 274 per square mile (106 per sq. km), is less than half that of Germany or the UK, but over three times that of the USA.

CLIMATE AND WEATHER

Hungary is said to have a temperate climate, but you could be fooled sometimes. The variability of the weather is explained by the position of the country, at the junction of the Maritime, Continental, and Mediterranean climatic zones. There seems to be a trend toward greater variation within the country, and from year to year, in both temperature and rainfall.

Most parts of Hungary have a mean annual temperature of between 50° and 52°F (10°–11°C), though in the last decade the areas exceeding 11°C have increased, particularly in the south of Hungary. The mean temperature is hottest in July (69°F, 20.5°C) and coldest in January (30°F, -1°C), but these averages may include hot days at 90°–104°F (33°–40°C) and cold nights at -15°–20°F (-26°–29°C), respectively. Local mean monthly temperatures in 2015 ranged between 23°F (-5.0°C) in January in the northern hills to 75°F (24°C) in the southeast during July and

August. The trend over the last forty years has been slightly upward, in line with global warming. The six months between September 2015 and March 2016 saw record high temperatures set on numerous days across the country.

Rainfall is variable too. The annual mean ranges from 28–32 inches (700–800 mm) in the west to 18–22 inches (470–550 mm) in the Great Plain. Yet 1999's nationwide mean of 31 inches (775 mm) was followed in 2000 by only 16 inches (400 mm). The pattern of rainfall is far from ideal. Much of it comes in summer thunder storms, so it quickly runs off or evaporates. This leaves parts of the Great Plain arid, with some shifting sand dunes to the west of Kecskemét.

Snow rarely falls before November or after April. A continuous period of snow cover and daytime frost is likely in December, January, and/or February.

Many Hungarians suffer from headaches or other symptoms as warm or cold weather fronts pass over.

The prevailing wind in Hungary is from the northwest. There are about 2,000 hours of sunshine a year

A BRIEF HISTORY
Before the Hungarians
The first written references to the area known as Hungary today date from the fifth century BCE. These, and archaeological evidence, suggest that Celtic tribes arrived about 400 BCE and controlled the area of modern Transdanubia—Hungary to the west of the Danube. Celtic culture in Hungary is thought to have been at its height toward the end of the third and into the second century BCE.

Rivalry with Illyrian, Dacian, and other tribes weakened the Celts. By about 12 BCE the Romans had established their rule over the area of modern western Hungary, which became part of the Roman province of Pannonia. There are some spectacular Roman remains, for example in Budapest (Aquincum) and near Székesfehérvár (Gorsium).

In 361 CE the Romans, their empire in decline, invited the troublesome, warlike Huns to settle in Pannonia, but the rule of their famous leader Attila was brief. There followed successive conquests of the area over more than five centuries by Ostrogoths, Gepids, Lombards, Avars, and Slavs, before the Hungarians arrived.

The Magyars
With no written historical records for guidance, it is hard to say exactly where the Magyars, or Hungarians, came from. Linguistically, Hungarian belongs to the Finno-Ugric group of languages (see page 156), the other surviving members of which occur in Northern Scandinavia and in pockets around the Baltic and across the territory of present-day Russia.

The split between the Finnic and Ugric tribes is usually dated to around 500 BCE, by which time the latter were pursuing an agricultural as well as a pastoral lifestyle, breeding horses and using iron. Their cultures were strongly influenced during the first millennium CE by tribes of Iranian origin and by neighboring Greek, Persian, and Armenian cultures.

By the fifth century CE, the Hungarians can be distinguished from other Ugric tribes and were in close contact with Bulgar Turks, on the steppes flanking the Volga River. They were part of successive loose federations of tribes, notably the Khazars.

By the ninth century, the Hungarians were centered further west around the Dnieper River and taking part in the political struggles among the Slavs and the Eastern Franks for control of the middle Danube Basin. They do not seem to have met any effective resistance when they invaded the Carpathian Basin at the end of the ninth century, united under Árpád, chief of the Magyar tribe. (Traditionally, seven tribes of warlike, pagan, seminomadic Magyars, headed by Árpád, are said to have crossed the Verecke Pass into the Carpathian Basin in 895 or 896, having lost their lands on the steppes of modern Ukraine to a Turkic tribe called the Pechenegs.)

The Avar empire of the previous century had been crushed by the Frankish forces of Charlemagne. Slav tribes predominated for a while, but the instability in the region prevented their states from consolidating. So about 400,000 Hungarians may have arrived in the Carpathian Basin, to find a local population of about 200,000, which seems to have been rapidly absorbed.

The Hungarians, still pagan and illiterate at this time, rivaled the earlier Vikings in the way they raided and pillaged much of Europe over the next sixty years. The "arrows of the Hungarians" feature as a terrorist scenario in many early chronicles. So Europe breathed a collective sigh of relief when military defeats persuaded the Hungarian ruling prince, Géza, in about 970 to prepare his country for the feudal Christian monarchy that his son and successor, King Stephen, founded.

Medieval Kingdom

The kingdom of Hungary came into being at Christmas in the year 1000, when Stephen I was crowned at Esztergom with a crown sent by Pope

Sylvester II. Some people have interpreted the gift to mean that Stephen owed his crown to God, not Mammon—the Holy Roman Empire centered in modern Germany, which was the main power in Europe at the time. In fact, Sylvester and Emperor Otto III were collaborating to consolidate Christianity and extend Christendom eastward in a political and religious sense. Stephen (István) was canonized in 1083.

By the time Stephen came to the throne, the Hungarians (Magyars) had been living in the Carpathian Basin for over a century and raiding in Europe for some time before that. Although medieval Hungary was almost completely devastated by Mongol incursions in 1241–2, it covered vast areas of central and southeastern Europe at various times. Buda became a center of the Renaissance under King Matthias I (1458–90), who amassed a famous library, second in size only to the Vatican's, and expanded the royal palace. Extensive remains of a summer palace can be seen at Visegrád, north of Budapest, strategically placed, overlooking the Danube Bend.

Partition

The reversal was rapid. Hungary was disastrously defeated by the Ottoman Turks in the battle of Mohács in 1526, and the fleeing Louis II, king of Hungary and Bohemia, was drowned in a stream. Buda, the royal capital, fell in 1541. Thereafter, "Royal Hungary" (the north and west) was ruled by Habsburg king-emperors from Vienna, while Central Hungary became a Turkish *sandjak* (province) under the pasha of Buda, and Transylvania a semi-independent principality—a haven of high cultural standards and religious toleration. Intermittent warfare between the Ottoman and Habsburg dominions continued.

Ottoman power in Hungary ended even more suddenly than it had begun. One moment Grand Vizir Kara Mustafa was boldly laying siege to Vienna in 1683, and the next he was suffering a succession of defeats. Buda was captured by Christian forces in 1686 and the Turks were ousted completely and irreversibly from Hungary by the 1699 Treaty of Karlowitz.

The legacy of the Ottoman period was mixed. The Turks had taxed the Hungarians hard, but they had

left the towns to run their own affairs. Also, they
had shown toleration toward Roman Catholicism,
Protestantism, and Judaism, whereas the Habsburgs
reimposed Catholicism by force.

The country was in a sorry, depopulated state
in the late seventeenth century, but this was due as
much to the warfare as to Ottoman misrule. There
were few left to rejoice when Buda was captured.
The combined Christian forces under Charles V,
Duke of Lorraine, marked the occasion by sacking
the city and conducting a pogrom against the Jews.

Modern Times

Nonetheless, Habsburg rule allowed Hungary to
begin moving toward modern Europe. There was
a long but abortive war of national independence
(1703–11) under Prince Ferenc Rákóczi II of
Transylvania, and relative prosperity did not come
until the 1720s. Varying degrees of Hungarian
autonomy followed.

Hungary, until the end of the First World War,
included modern Slovakia, Sub-Carpathian Ukraine,
Transylvania (now in Romania), Vojvodina (now

in Serbia), most of Croatia, and the future Austrian province of Burgenland. Agriculture benefited in the eighteenth century from Imperial rule tempered by a Diet (legislative assembly) of nobles, usually meeting in Pozsony (Pressburg, modern Bratislava). But a truly modern economy and society based on commerce, industry, education, and toleration came later than it did in Germany, Italy, or France.

Only in 1805 did officialdom begin to use Hungarian alongside Latin, which survived as the language spoken in the Diet until 1832. But Hungarian development was unusual, as it was led by the lower nobility and gentry, resentful of aristocratic power, rather than by a bourgeoisie. Acceleration of development in the 1830s and '40s culminated in a bloodless revolution in Buda and Pest in March 1848, led by Lajos Kossuth. Inspired by similar events in Paris and Vienna, the reformists declared Hungary's autonomy within the Habsburg Empire. The subsequent war of independence was crushed by the Habsburgs the following year, with assistance from Tsarist Russia.

Many reforms were reversed, and harsh direct rule from Vienna continued for almost twenty years. Eventually, in 1867 the *Ausgleich*, or Compromise, brokered between the Hungarian nobility and the imperial court, created the Dual Austro-Hungarian Monarchy, in which Austria and Hungary had separate governments. This curious arrangement precipitated a forty-year spurt of belated bourgeois development—political, economic, and social development that set its mark on Budapest (created by a merger of Buda, Pest, and Óbuda in 1876) and made it the fastest-growing capital in Europe after Berlin.

Independence and Occupation

Hungary at last gained full independence after the First World War, but it lost 71 percent of its territory and 63 percent of its population under the 1920 Treaty of Trianon, imposed at the Versailles peace conference. Sizeable Hungarian minorities are still found across the borders in Slovakia, Romania, and Serbia, as well as smaller communities in Ukraine, Croatia, Slovenia, and Austria.

After a 133-day Communist interlude in 1919, independent Hungary became a nominal kingdom

again. It was headed from 1920 to 1944 by a regent, Miklós Horthy, previously a rear admiral in the Austro-Hungarian navy, although Charles IV of Habsburg made two, somewhat naïve and bungled, attempts to regain his throne in 1921.

But Horthy remained. He and successive conservative, irredentist governments he appointed aligned the country with Italy and Germany, in return for what turned out to be very temporary territorial gains in the late 1930s and early 1940s. Rampant anti-Semitism came after German military occupation in March 1944, followed by a German-engineered *coup d'état* in October. Some 600,000 Hungarian Jews were sent to death camps, along with large numbers of Gypsies.

The Soviet army that defeated the German and Hungarian forces in 1944–5 was ill-disciplined, and the reprisals were severe. Huge reparations had to be paid. About half a million Hungarians were deported to labor camps in the Soviet Union, from which many never returned. Initially, Hungary had its own democratic government alongside a Soviet-dominated Allied Control Commission, but the Communists undermined it, gaining power and imposing a classic Communist regime.

Stalinist rule under the local dictator Mátyás Rákosi brought oppression, upheaval, and impossible economic strains. Faced with the imminent collapse of its satellite state, Khrushchev's Russia in 1953 supported the installation of a reformist government under Imre Nagy, but then

the Kremlin vacillated, allowing Rákosi to return.
This led during 1956 to mounting protest and
finally rebellion.

The '56 Revolution
The sight of Soviet tanks firing into crowds in a
Communist satellite country shook the world in October
1956. If the Suez Crisis and the invasion of Egypt hadn't
distracted the world's attention from Hungary there
might conceivably have been UN intervention, as the
Hungarian revolutionaries were hoping.

By 1956 came a thaw, and ideas for reform were
being openly discussed. However, the uprising, when
it came, was sudden and unforeseen. On October 22,
a student rally at Budapest Technical University listed
sixteen demands, including free elections, withdrawal
of Soviet troops, and higher pay.

On October 23, a student march, ostensibly in
support of Polish protestors, was joined spontaneously
by workers and employees. By evening, 200,000 people
were standing before Parliament, as a crowd elsewhere
in the city toppled the giant statue of Stalin, and
another crowd outside the Radio was calling angrily

for the Sixteen Points to be broadcast. The Hungarian Communist Party leadership appointed Imre Nagy to head a new government. The Radio was stormed, and the first Soviet troops to enter the capital the next morning met armed resistance. Most units of the Hungarian army stood aside, while many officers and men went over to the freedom fighters.

By October 26, there was a general strike. Revolutionary councils in communities and factories were in control, demanding Soviet withdrawal and a neutral, democratic, independent Hungary. The revolution spread to other cities, where Soviet units were confronted by rebels, and Hungarian army units stood aside.

Initially concerned to appease the Soviets, the Western Powers plucked up courage on October 27 and called on the UN Security Council to debate the situation. On the night of October 27–8, a ceasefire was brokered, Soviet troops withdrew from Budapest, and negotiations started on Soviet withdrawal. But this Communist-brokered deal foundered, partly because the revolutionaries refused to disarm or go back to work. In addition, news of a few dozen ugly

public lynchings of suspected Communist officials probably influenced Kremlin thinking.

A Soviet decision to crush the uprising and replace the reformist government was made in Moscow on the night of October 30–31 and carried out on November 4. The Nagy government took refuge in the Yugoslav embassy as the tanks rolled in, but its members refused to resign in favor of a puppet regime under János Kádár, which was sworn in on November 7.

Sporadic fighting continued until November 11, and political and civil resistance into the new year. The UN General Assembly confined itself to condemning the Soviet aggression.

Kádár made initial concessions and promised an amnesty, but over the next three years the Communist reprisals and terror led to 13,000 people being interned, over 20,000 imprisoned, and some 230 executed, Nagy and other senior figures among them. Most prisoners were released in a 1963 amnesty, but several were held until the mid-1970s. Many were never allowed to work in their occupations again. About 200,000 Hungarians, the majority young and male, fled into exile.

Reprisals and Reforms
Perhaps it is not too fanciful to draw parallels between the long Kádár period (1956–89) and the period of direct Habsburg rule (1849–67). Both were initially brutal. Both were absolutist, though in some degree enlightened. Each rested on a small elite of questionable legitimacy or suitability for running a modern state.

Kádár's Hungary tinkered with the Soviet model and sought to promote economic and political détente with the West, a process that accelerated in the 1980s. The reforms it introduced culminated in a voluntary abdication of power in 1989–90.

Communism had been costly to maintain, and what with the high price of conversion to capitalism, Hungary had foreign debts that peaked in 1995 at 84 percent of the annual economic output (GDP). Some longer-term social effects of the Communist period are discussed in Chapter 2.

Change of System
The collapse of Communism and transformation of a Soviet satellite country into an independent parliamentary democracy with a fast-growing market economy is known in Hungary as the "change of system" (*rendszerváltás*).

Hungary passed the big tests in the economic and political spheres. Economically—with at least some of the early steps already begun—it went for a gradual approach, rather than the "shock therapy" preferred in several other post-Communist countries, where most of the state assets were given away to the public.

In the first five years of the democratic era the country suffered economically as outdated, inefficient, and overstaffed industries and institutions were closed down. Between 1990 and 2010, successive Hungarian governments put great efforts into establishing the institutions and rule of law essential if a modern economy is to thrive, if not always with complete success.

The election in 2010 of the right-wing Viktor Orbán as prime minister resulted in massive legislative upheaval—designed to restore full Hungarian independence and eliminate subservience to, among others, Brussels and Western bankers.

Critics, however, counter that the changes have removed the checks and balances needed in state institutions, undermining the rule of law in Hungary, and paving the way for future election victories for the incumbents by dint of their control of most of the media.

Orbán is also accused of seeking to win the far-right vote by rehabilitating anti-Semitic historical figures and promoting a right-wing view of history.

Furthermore, while the gap between rich and poor opened up in the first two decades of the transition—leading to public nostalgia for the perceived certainty of the Kádár era—Orbán's economic policies have further widened it. The government has not addressed the real problems of the growing underclass. And while there is some prosperity based on low-cost manufacturing and shared service centers, critics say rampant corruption and cronyism means the benefits flow to a narrow range of favored supporters and family surrounding the prime minister.

Eleven centuries after arriving in Central Europe, the Hungarians acceded to the European Union on May 1, 2004. But the path from one entry to the other had not been smooth. A decade or so after accession, for many Hungarians it has not got any easier.

GOVERNMENT

Hungary is a parliamentary democracy with a non-executive head of state, so that executive power is in the hands of the government, headed by the prime minister.

Parliament (officially the National Assembly) has a single chamber with members elected by all citizens

over the age of eighteen except for those specifically barred from doing so, such as criminals.

Under a new electoral law, controversially adopted in 2011, the new, slimmed-down parliament consists of 199 seats in total (down from 386 in the parliaments from 1990 to 2010), with 106 representatives elected via single constituencies and 93 via party lists.

Parties must win 5 percent of the aggregate list votes to qualify for any list seats in Parliament at all. Citizens resident in Hungary have two votes in a one-round election (previously it was two rounds), one for their resident constituency, the second for the party list. The new election law also allows non-resident citizens to vote, but only on the party list.

The head of state is the president of the republic, who is elected for a five-year term by a two-thirds majority of Parliament. The president has to sign all parliamentary legislation and has limited powers to delay it, refer it back for reconsideration, or submit it to the Constitutional Court for a ruling.

He (at present) also has powers to initiate legislation and issue judicial pardons. The president resides and works in a modest palace on Castle Hill. Plans envisage the Prime Minister's Office and residence to be relocated to Castle Hill in 2017–18.

Parliament elects the prime minister by a simple majority and has to approve his government. (There has not been a female prime minister so far.) General elections are held every four years. At present, local elections are held in the first year of each new government term.

POLITICS

The first free general elections in 1990 resulted in a center-right coalition, led by the Hungarian Democratic Forum (MDF). Each of the elections thereafter turned out an incumbent government, a pattern first broken in 2006, when the Socialist–Free Democrat (liberal) coalition was reelected.

However, relations between the governing coalition parties soured and finally collapsed, with a Socialist-backed technocrat government heading the country as it struggled to negotiate the effects of global economic crisis in 2009–10.

In 2010, Fidesz (see page 32) led by Viktor Orbán, won a landslide victory in the Spring elections. While previous elections had typically resulted in numerous dismissals of officials and functionaries as the new government maneuvered its own people into all crucial and/or lucrative positions, the new Orbán government initiated massive changes in administration at all levels, usually with little or no consultation.

Parliament is often sparsely attended and dogged by ill temper and insults. Cooperation between the government and the opposition is minimal. Libel suits involving politicians are frequent and protracted. These aspects, coupled with widespread evidence of corruption and cronyism, have eroded the overall public reputation of politics and politicians.

Parliament elects, with a two-thirds majority, the fifteen members of the Constitutional Court, who sit for twelve-year terms and rule on whether legislation is constitutional or not. Until 2010, it was typically extremely difficult to find nonpartisan candidates capable of attaining this threshold support. Similar problems arose with electing ombudsmen, the head of the national audit authority, and the chief justice. But with Viktor Orbán's sweeping victories in the 2010 and 2014 elections, the two-thirds so-called "super majority" was guaranteed, the result being that the opposition accused the prime minister of stuffing these nominally non-partisan posts with Fidesz loyalists. The Constitutional Court has now had its powers curbed. (The government subsequently lost its two-thirds majority as a result of defeat in two by-elections in 2015. However, most observers believe it could still garner support via the votes of far-right MPs if necessary.)

Similarly, esteem for the audit authority and the prosecution service has declined—the latter in particular as a result of turning a blind eye to seemingly incontrovertible evidence of corruption in Budapest District V over the sale of prime real estate to political friends at knock-down prices.

HUNGARY'S GOVERNING AND PRINCIPAL POLITICAL PARTIES

The "Fidesz government"

Strictly speaking, Viktor Orbán is head of the Fidesz–Hungarian Civic Union party. In practice, the party is referred to simply as "Fidesz" 99 percent of the time. Fidesz considers itself a "conservative" party, similar to the Christian Democratic Union of Germany, and is a member of the European Peoples' Party grouping in the European Parliament.

Technically, Orbán is prime minister of a coalition government comprising Fidesz and the Christian Democratic Peoples' Party (Hungarian acronym, KDNP). In the 2014 election, Fidesz won 117 seats, against 16 for the KDNP. In real life, nobody believes the KDNP is anything but a Fidesz front, created and maintained to enhance Fidesz's power, for example in parliamentary committees, and by attracting more official state funding. Hence the administration is simply termed "the Fidesz government" in daily practice.

The Socialist Party (MszP)

This is the traditional center-left party and legal inheritor of the Socialist Workers' Party (MSZMP)—generally termed the "Communist Party" from 1956 to 1989. It has struggled to recover from the 2010 election defeat and subsequent secession of the Democratic Coalition faction.

Movement for a Better Hungary (Jobbik)
Founded in 2003, Jobbik gained popularity
with a nationalist, anti-Semitic, and anti-Roma
agenda, winning over 20 percent of the vote
in the 2014 elections. However, since then its
leader, Gábor Vona, has forced the party to take
a more moderate line.

Democratic Coalition (DK)
A social-democratic grouping formed by a
breakaway group from the Socialist Party in
2011 under the leadership of Ferenc Gyurcsány,
prime minister from 2004 to 2009.

Politics can be Different (LMP)
Founded as a green party, with a vein of
national-conservatism helping it to win
conservatives who dislike Fidesz.

Dialogue for Hungary
A splinter group from LMP, founded because
it deemed an electoral alliance with the left-
democratic parties as the only pragmatic way
to fight the 2014 election. LMP steadfastly, or
stubbornly, would only stand alone.

Together-Party for a New Era
Another small, centrist democratic grouping.

Hungarian Liberal Party
Comprises just one MP, achieved via the 2014
electoral alliance.

For now, the judiciary is generally trusted, despite the removal of many older (and therefore more likely independent) judges. Respect for politicians, however, seems to be at an all-time low, although such loss of prestige is not peculiar to Hungary.

THE ECONOMY

In the first years of the democratic era, Hungary made great strides from a centrally planned economy to one based on market principles. Indeed, up to about 1997 Hungary was widely touted as the regional leader in the transition stakes.

However, for many these were painful years. Numerous state companies, previously protected by Comecom trade barriers, were unable to compete with better-value foreign imports. If they didn't shut them down, the state privatized many other ailing enterprises, including energy and water utilities, both to raise funds for the budget and to attract modern management know-how for desperately needed modernization.

The turmoil produced mass redundancies, deep recession, and controversies, with many Hungarians convinced the state had sold off "the family silver." Somewhat ironically, it was the Socialist–liberal coalition of 1994–98 that forced through the most radical market reforms, resulting in economic growth of 3.5–4.5 percent from 1997 for some years onward, mostly driven by foreign direct investment into manufacturing companies.

So much so that by the turn of the millennium Hungary had attracted scores of manufacturing companies from North America, Western Europe, and Asia, including global brand names such as Alcoa, GE, General Motors, IBM, Guardian Glass, Philips, Electrolux, Audi, and Suzuki.

However, privatization and the market reform processes slowed down—and in some cases were reversed—under supposedly conservative Fidesz governments between 1998 and 2002, and most especially post-2010, when the state controversially renationalized the mandatory private pension funds, most utilities, several banks, and an assortment of other companies.

The Impact of the Global Crisis
The changed outlook was in part brought on by the 2008–09 world economic crisis, which hit Hungary hard. As exports plunged, hundreds of small firms, especially in services and hospitality, failed to survive. Hundreds of thousands of households that had taken out foreign-currency denominated loans (mostly in Swiss francs) were simultaneously struck by increasing monthly debt repayments as the forint sank in value.

In the fall of 2008, Hungary called in the IMF as bond investors looked as if they would no longer finance Hungary's bloated budget deficit. The economy contracted by 6.5 percent in 2009, and although it bottomed out and began to grow slowly in the second half of that year, many Hungarians felt aggrieved with the system, giving Viktor Orbán's Fidesz party a landslide victory in the 2010 elections.

Based primarily on the return to (albeit sluggish) growth in Germany, which supported manufacturing exports, and a huge government drive to win European Union funds, the economy expanded by 3 to 3.5 percent in 2014–15, and looks set to grow by 2 to 3 percent for some years to come. With the current account balance at record positive levels and unemployment officially down to 5.5 percent in mid-2016, the government is keen to boast it has turned the economy onto a successful, sustainable growth path.

It all looks very positive. However, independent economists warn that the macro figures are deceptive: if the EU funds are stripped out of the equation, then GDP growth would be non-existent. Further, the unemployment figures have been boosted partly by employment abroad (but still counted statistically as domestic) and partly by public works schemes, which have taken some 200,000 unskilled workers off the books, but which are not effective in preparing these people for real employment in the marketplace.

In addition, while the Orbán governments have been almost fixated on keeping the budget deficit at below 3 percent, the austerity measures (for that is what they were, despite repeated denials by the government) enacted in 2010–14 to help achieve this have left tens of thousands in the social services, health, and education sectors on miserable official salaries and very disgruntled.

Not only public service workers felt the pinch. Emigration has soared since 2010, with an estimated 500,000–600,000 Hungarians in total working abroad by 2016, the UK, Germany, and Austria being the favored locations. With many of these emigrés well-educated, as the economy began to pick up, by 2014 employers began complaining of a shortage of both skilled and unskilled labor, from waiters to engineers.

After a fruitless effort to lure these expats home by offering financial incentives, in mid-2016 the government agreed to allow some non-EU immigration into the country on a "temporary" basis in an attempt to solve the labor shortage. Whether this is successful remains to be seen. Whatever the outcome, government efforts to address this issue—while avoiding wage inflation and a loss of competitiveness—will be a major challenge for the next decade.

BUDAPEST

The capital of Hungary dominates the country far more thoroughly than Vienna dominates Austria or London the United Kingdom. For a start, look at a map of Hungary. All the main roads and highways radiate from Budapest.

One can demonstrate this in economic terms. Budapest, where 18 percent of Hungary's population live and/or work, accounts for 39 percent of its economic output (GDP).

This dominance is nothing new. The Castle of Buda (Budavár), overlooking Óbuda, was the royal seat and capital of Hungary for most of the Middle Ages, although some kings based themselves at Esztergom, Székesfehérvár, or Visegrád. Central Hungary under the Ottoman Empire was controlled by the pasha of Buda, while the Habsburg regions of the divided country were ruled from Pozsony (Bratislava, capital of Slovakia) and the Transylvanian princes held court at Kolozsvár (today's Cluj-Napoca in Romania). Pozsony remained the usual place for the assembly of nobles to meet, but its slim pretensions to be a capital ended in the Revolution of 1848.

By that time, Pest and Buda, on the left and right banks of the Danube respectively, made up the country's main urban area, but Hungary was still dominated by the countryside and agriculture, not its towns. Rapid development of the capital began after the *Ausgleich* of 1867 and the union of Pest, Buda, and Óbuda as Budapest in 1876. By the end of the century, Budapest had 717,681 inhabitants.

Hungary's territorial losses after the First World War accentuated the dominance of Budapest. Such cities as Pozsony (Bratislava) and Kassa (Košice) were ceded to Czechoslovakia, Kolozsvár (Cluj-Napoca),

and Temesvár (Timişoara) to Romania, and Újvidék (Novi Sad) to the new Yugoslav kingdom. Several surrounding towns and villages were merged into Budapest in 1948, creating a city of 1.6 million inhabitants.

Budapest today has a population of about 1.7 million, with an official conurbation of 3.3 million. (The next-largest city, Debrecen, has only 200,000 inhabitants.) The capital is run by its municipality under an elected chief mayor and a thirty-three-member assembly. The city is divided into twenty-three districts, each of which has a similar structure of mayor and assembly. An uneasy, rather arbitrary, division of labor has emerged between the municipality and the district governments.

The Danube, here 1,000–2,000 feet (300–600 m) wide, runs between the steep hills of Buda and the

plains of Pest. The views are stunning from both sides, as many of the city's main buildings can be seen from the banks—Parliament, the Royal Palace of Buda, and the Buda Castle District, the towers and domes of the main churches, the Academy of Sciences, the Gresham Palace, and other great nineteenth-century buildings. This is a UNESCO World Heritage site.

Moving downstream from north to south, the first main island in Budapest is Hajógyári (Shipyard) Island off Óbuda, scene of the congenial, internationally popular Sziget (Island) rock festival every summer. Traffic-free Margaret Island is the city's most attractive and popular public park, with swimming pools and a couple of hotels. Csepel Island, in the south of the city, accommodates the industrial District XXI of Budapest, as well as several other towns and villages.

Some Key Dates

35 BCE–433 CE Roman rule over Pannonia.

895–6 The Magyars began to settle in the Carpathian Basin, and made raids throughout Europe until 970. Transylvania colonized.

972–97 Prince Géza sent envoys to the Holy Roman Emperor and accepted Christian missionaries in Hungary.

1000–1038 Stephen (István) I, as first king, established a Western Christian feudal state.

1083 Stephen I, his son Emericus (Imre), and his evangelist, Bishop Gerard (Gellért), canonized.

1172–96 The reign of Béla III, under whom Hungary became a major power in the Balkans.

1192–5 The Pray Codex contained the "Funeral Oration," the earliest continuous Hungarian text.

1241–2 Hungary sacked by Mongol hordes.

1301 The royal House of Árpád died out with Andrew III. He was succeeded after six years' civil war by Charles (Károly) I of Anjou.

1342–82 Louis (Lajos) I conquered Dalmatia. He expelled the Jews from Hungary in 1360. He became king of Poland as well in 1370.

1433 Sigismund (Zsigmond) of Luxemburg, King of Hungary (since 1387, Bohemia since 1420, and Milan since 1431), crowned Holy Roman Emperor.

1456 Governor János Hunyadi defended Belgrade against the Ottoman Turks, halting their advance.

1458–90 King Matthias (Mátyás) I Corvinus centralized government. Hungary became a strong military power and cultural center.

1526 The battle of Mohács. Under Sulaiman the Magnificent the Turks defeated the Hungarians.

1541 Buda captured by the Turks.

1570 The Treaty of Speyer partitioned Hungary between the Ottoman and Habsburg empires, with Transylvania as a separate independent principality. Intermittent warfare.

1672 Rebellion against the Habsburgs escalated under Imre Thököly, who founded a Turkish-allied principality in north Hungary in 1678.

1686 Buda sacked after its recapture from the Turks by Christian forces. Thököly crushed.

1699 Hungary freed from the Turks by the Peace of Karlowitz, and reunited under Habsburg rule.

1703–11 Prince Ferenc Rákóczi II led a Hungarian uprising against Austria, forcing it to promise to respect the Hungarian constitution.

1722 The Pragmatic Sanction agreed upon between the Diet and the Habsburgs governed Hungary's constitutional relations to its kings.

1777 The *ratio educationis* law left the Churches to run the schools.

1809 Napoleon advanced from Vienna to Győr. The Hungarian *insurrectio*, or noble militia, was called out for the last time and lost the battle.

1825 Count István Széchenyi funded a Scholarly Society, forerunner of the Hungarian Academy of Sciences. Development in the Age of Reform.

1844 Hungarian became the official language, but less than half the population were Hungarian.

1848 European social and political unrest spread to Pest. Lajos Kossuth took the lead in the national revolution. The semifeudal Diet gave way to a National Assembly. Serfdom abolished by The March Laws. War broke out, but the Croats and others sided with Vienna.

1849 The National Assembly repudiated the Habsburgs and elected Kossuth head of state. Russia intervened on Austria's behalf and Hungary surrendered. Executions and direct rule ensued. Kossuth in exile promoted Hungary as an archetype of an oppressed nation.

1867 The *Ausgleich* (compromise) with the Habsburgs gave Hungary self-government, and equality with Austria within a dual monarchy. Economic and social development followed.

1868 The Education Act provided for six years of compulsory schooling in the local language, with state supervision. Emancipation of the Jews.

1914 Austria-Hungary declared war on Serbia, precipitating the First World War.

1918–19 Defeated, the Habsburg Empire broke up. A revolution on October 30, 1918, led by Count Mihály Károlyi, foundered over imposed territorial losses. A second revolution on March 21, 1919, installed a Communist regime under Béla Kun, but Czech and Romanian forces attacked and an army under Admiral Miklós Horthy seized power. Reprisals followed.

1920 Parliament elected Horthy regent. The *numerus clausus* law restricted the proportion of Jews in higher education and some professions. The Treaty of Trianon confirmed that Hungary could retain only 29 percent of its former territory with 37 percent of its population.

1932–6 Foreign policy under the Gömbös government swung Hungary behind the German–Italian Axis.

1938 The first Jewish law restricted Jewish employment. The Hitler-brokered First Vienna Award ceded parts of Slovakia to Hungary.

1939 Subcarpathia (Czechoslovak Ruthenia) ceded to Hungary. The second Jewish law defined Jews in racial terms, restricted political rights of Jews, and introduced labor service for "unreliable elements."

1940 The Second Vienna Award ceded north Transylvania to Hungary.

1941 Hungary joined the German attack on Yugoslavia and was rewarded with territory lost in 1920. War with the Soviet Union and Britain.

1943 The Hungarian Second Army annihilated at the Don Bend.

1944 German occupation installed a Nazi regime. Horthy failed to bail Hungary out of the war and resigned. Jewish deportation to death camps began. An interim legislature met in the Soviet-held city of Debrecen.

1945 Armistice. The Soviets expelled the last German forces. Hungary had lost a million people and 40 percent of its national wealth in the Second World War. Free general elections held.

1946 Communist influence steadily increased, helped by the Soviet-run Allied Control Commission. Hyperinflation is solved by currency reform and the introduction of the forint.

1946–8 Nationalization of the economy and education. The 1920 frontiers restored by treaty.

1948 A forced merger of the Communist and Social Democratic parties brought Soviet-style one-party dictatorship under Mátyás Rákosi. Living standards plummeted as resources diverted to heavy industry. Mass internment and relocation. Cardinal Mindszenty, head of the Catholic Church, among many show-trial victims.

1955 Reform-minded Communist Imre Nagy dismissed as prime minister. The Warsaw Pact created.

1956 Anti-Soviet uprising broke out in Budapest. Imre Nagy, recalled as prime minister, announced Hungary's withdrawal from the Warsaw Pact. Hopes of Western or UN assistance faded and Soviet forces returned to the capital, installing a quisling government under János Kádár.

1956–8 Brutal reprisals brought more than 200 executions, including that of Imre Nagy.

1959 Collectivization of agriculture completed.

1968 A New Economic Mechanism of "market socialism" introduced. Hungary assisted in the Soviet occupation of Czechoslovakia.

1978 The USA under President Jimmy Carter returned the Holy Crown and coronation regalia sent there after the Second World War.

1984 A visit by British Prime Minister Margaret Thatcher confirmed warmer relations with the West.

1987–8 Opposition groups formed openly. János Kádár dropped as head of the Communist Party.

1989 Roundtable Communist–opposition talks charted a course to multiparty democracy.

US President George Bush visited. Hungary opened its border with Austria for East German refugees to flee to the West, so breaching the Iron Curtain. A new republic was declared.

1990 Soviet occupation forces begin withdrawal. Elections produced a center-right coalition government that pursued radical free-market reforms.

1990–2000 A market economy was restored and mass privatization of state assets occurred.

1994 General elections produced a socialist–liberal coalition.

1995 Hungary joined the Organization for Economic Cooperation and Development (OECD). Visitors included US President Bill Clinton and Pope John Paul II.

1998 General elections brought a right-wing coalition led by Prime Minister Viktor Orbán.

1999 Hungary joined NATO and made facilities available for bombing Serbia. It later gave assistance to the US in Afghanistan and Iraq.

2002 General elections led to a socialist–liberal coalition.

2004 Hungary joined the EU.

2006 General election resulted in a continuation of socialist –liberal coalition. In September, news breaks of the infamous "We have lied night and day" speech by Prime Minister Ferenc Gyurcsány at a closed party meeting. This results in unprecedented riots in Budapest, and a storming of the state TV building.

2008 Hungary requests emergency loan worth €20 million from the IMF in the wake of economic global crisis.

2010 Viktor Orbán and Fidesz win a "super" two-thirds majority in parliament. Jobbik, the radical right-wing party, is the third largest party in parliament, with 23 seats.

The new parliament begins a frenzy of law-making, along with controversial "emergency taxes" that largely hit foreign-owned companies.

2012 The new "Fundamental Law" or constitution, comes into force.

Malév, the Hungarian national airline, collapses.

President Pál Schmitt, in office since 2010, resigns after media reports that he had plagiarized his doctoral dissertation.

2014 The government signs up to controversial plans for a new, €12bn Russian-designed nuclear power station, mainly financed from Moscow.

Viktor Orbán wins a second two-thirds majority in parliamentary elections, under a new, single-round election system.

Street protests over a proposed Internet tax force the government to back down.

2015 The "Simicska Break." Lajos Simicska, previously considered Viktor Orbán's most trusted supporter in terms of business and media, publicly breaks with the prime minister with expletive-ridden statements.

The refugee–migrant "crisis." Hungary erects a controversial fence along its southern border with Serbia and Croatia to deter asylum seekers, mostly from the war-torn Middle East.

Critics accuse Hungary of conducting a hate campaign against migrants and of flouting international law on asylum seekers. Prime Minister Orbán insists that his first duty is to protect the EU's Schengen border, and says Hungary opposes mass migration.

2016 Viktor Orbán, as part of a general attack on the European Union, initiates a referendum on whether to accept EU plans to mandate resettlement of refugees. Following a massive government campaign, 98 percent of voters voted "no" in line with government wishes, but the referendum is invalid, failing to reach the required 50 percent turnout of the electorate.

Népszabadság, the main opposition newspaper, is closed down by its Austrian owner, ostensibly for commercial reasons. Shortly after, the Austrian owner sells its remaining portfolio, including twelve regional dailies, to a company widely believed to be close to the government.

PISA assessment reveals Hungarian educational standards in science and reading comprehension have slid further. This comes on top of a weakening performance in the 2013 assessment.

chapter two

VALUES &
ATTITUDES

Hungary entered the twenty-first century on a high. After grappling with the shock of the collapse of Comecon—the protected Communist version of a "common market"—its economy was humming and the country was well on the road to membership of the European Union. National pride was feeling satisfied. Hungary had an image in the outside world that it could live with—or even play up to. Though some parts of that image might be random or even misplaced, many have embedded themselves as virtues to be cultivated and displayed.

However, the 2008 global crisis hit Hungary hard, and disenchantment with the Socialist–liberal government became widespread. The political upheavals that followed the election of Viktor Orbán as prime minister in 2010 have divided the nation: for some, the image has become more the reality, for others it is badly sullied. Behind these images lie values and attitudes that visiting tourists, business folk, or journalists are less likely to know in advance.

IMAGE AND SELF-IMAGE

Just as there's brave little Belgium in Western Europe, so there's brave little Hungary in Central Europe. (Central Europe, with its cultural echoes of *Mitteleuropa*, is seen as preferable as a designation to Eastern Europe, with its overtones of the drab Soviet period.) Hungarians earned that reputation as a brave, beleaguered people in sixteenth- to nineteenth-century wars against the Ottoman and Habsburg empires. It was regained in the twentieth century, through the 1945–90 Soviet occupation, and especially the defiance shown in the 1956 Revolution.

But there are other, deep, Hungarian historical grievances. The deepest is the Treaty of Trianon, which truncated the country after the First World War. Such resentments are perplexing and even distasteful to outsiders, rather as Irish national grievances can seem to British people. But just as few Irishmen aspire to let off bombs in Belfast these days, so few Hungarians seriously contemplate revising the country's Trianon borders. Yet the grievance lives on, as part of a feeling of national melancholy. Hungarians still feel bloodied but unbowed.

At this point, it must be said that Hungary has a different image in Central and Eastern Europe from the one it has in the rest of the world. Just as Hungarians are often resentful of neighboring countries, so neighboring peoples are often resentful of Hungary, which in their eyes does not have the proudest of records with regard to the nationalities it once ruled over.

Today, the Hungarian minority communities in the midst of the successor countries are sometimes the focus of controversy. The sometimes mutual resentment applies in varying degrees, of course: more strongly in Slovakia, Romania, and Serbia; hardly at all in Austria, Croatia, or Slovenia.

One difference between the two images of Hungary is in the degree of familiarity they reflect.

While some in neighboring countries certainly remain suspicious of Budapest's intentions, most of the millions of tourists visiting Hungary today have an overwhelmingly positive experience. They are typically impressed by the cultural offerings, museums, restaurant life, local transportation, and the safe streets. For those who get to the countryside, the Baroque splendor of the churches, and the joviality of local wine and other festivals make for lasting, fond memories.

CULTURE

While neighboring Central European peoples often see nationalism as a Hungarian characteristic and a potential threat, those Western Europeans and North Americans who have an image of Hungarians at all are likely to see them as cultured, hospitable, vivacious, and resourceful. Now there's an image worth living up to, as many Hungarians realize.

Factors behind the "cultured" perception include the contribution that Hungarians like Alexander Korda and George Cukor made to the film industry between the

1930s and the 1960s, and composers such as Liszt, Kálmán, Lehár, Dohnányi, Bartók, and Kodály, and the conductor Sir Georg Solti, made to music in the nineteenth and twentieth centuries.

But are Hungarians more cultured or educated than most? It's safe to say that Hungarian *gymnasia* (academically oriented secondary schools) make greater demands on their students than English comprehensives or American high schools do. Family expectations of middle-class children are higher too.

As an illustration of what the *gymnasium* system has been able to do, Hungarians often boast that the country has more Nobel Prizewinners per capita than any other nation. Some sources claim as many as eighteen, although thirteen looks to be the more frequently cited figure—neither of which is bad for a country today of 10 million. (In truth, this claim is difficult to pin down, not least because it is very difficult to define nationality in a region with mixed—and moving—populations. Certainly almost all those Nobel Laureates received their awards living outside present-day Hungary.) But, regardless of the exact definitions and numbers, Hungarian-born scientists, engineers, physicians, and innovators have undoubtedly contributed to mankind's development in numerous fields.

Not that all teenagers go to *gymnasia*. An increasing number attend vocational secondary schools, although these sometimes provide a low standard of general education alongside dubious or obsolete vocational skills. The government has given assurances that it is addressing these needs.

THE AFTERMATH OF COMMUNISM

More than twenty-five years have gone by since Hungary emerged in 1989–90 from forty years of totalitarian Communist rule, four decades that have strongly influenced how Hungarians relate to each other and how they see themselves.

The Communist regime, headed after 1956 by János Kádár, built up a stock of goodwill in the West in the 1970s and 1980s, with a more jovial, consumerist brand of "Goulash Communism." It ran its economy rather differently from Russia's, so that there were no breadlines. Hungary was seen as the Soviet satellite prepared to sail closest to the wind with its initiatives to improve East–West relations—as the Soviet Union's stalking horse, of course. And the Kádár regime liked to present an *avant-garde* image in the arts as well.

FEARS AND CHANCES

Kádár and his handpicked elite presented themselves as benevolent tacticians, allowing the Hungarians to get away with as much as possible without upsetting their masters in Moscow. Fear of Moscow was one factor, certainly, but there was another: fear of their own people. Nobody would want another bloody, bitter '56 Revolution. From the 1960s onward, as it became increasingly clear that they could not deliver as well as the (supposedly despised) West, many Communists were becoming cynical about their own beliefs.

Indeed, Hungary's well-placed Communist Party members were gratified to find they could act as a political and economic elite that did very well for itself, and if the price was lip service to Communism, so be it. Many Hungarians today suspect that members of the same ex-Communist elite did very well later, too, out of post-Communist privatization.

But the Communist system, even in its superficially humanized, marketized Hungarian version, was the most extensively totalitarian system the world had ever known. Nazism and fascism might have outdone Communism in savagery, but the Communist system won on breadth and comprehensiveness. It did not just cover government and local government, the organizations of society and politics, the armed forces, and the education system, as fascism did. It annihilated or annexed all civil initiative and held absolute sway over the economy.

That applied also in Hungary, even if Kádár's regime toyed with the idea of granting freedom of action to some members of the Communist elite—in their guise as company managers—to respond to limited, distorted market forces, if they felt so inclined. If they didn't feel so inclined, they could join the crowd of other managers of state-owned "enterprises," as the corporations were called, pleading for special treatment and extra state funds. There was little risk involved. Just one major firm (in the construction industry) was allowed to go bust under the Kádár regime. All the other loss makers were bailed out, time and time again.

WORK ETHIC

Communism ruined the work ethic: productivity was low, and the standing joke was "You pretend to pay us and we pretend to work." It was common to have another one or two jobs on top of the "official" position, and use official work time and assets for the "entrepreneurial" extra jobs. (This practice caught out some foreign investors in the 1990s, when the local workforce was found to be eager to earn Western salaries, but less eager to work the expected hours.) Properly managed, however, the Hungarian workforce can be as productive as the best (see pages 143–44).

Intriguingly, the appearance of growing wealth of well-connected individuals during Communist times was greeted with a sullen acceptance by the masses— rather, indeed, as it is today. Under Kádár—who was, himself, a very modest man in terms of lifestyle—the public flaunting of wealth (and certainly by Party members) was discouraged. That inhibition is less apparent today, when a Mercedes driver may well pull up, jump out and walk past a gaggle of homeless compatriots to shop for luxuries in a supermarket. The street dwellers, however, will barely notice: should they do so, they will merely shrug their shoulders in silent acquiesence. Such attitudes permeate society.

HIERARCHY AND STATUS

While the culture in society in general, and in many modern companies, is far more relaxed than before 1990, that does not make Hungary a country where you greet a visiting executive with "high-fives."

As in much of the European continent (certainly anywhere with a historic German influence), titles and educational achievements are often up front—with Dr., M.A., M.S./M.Sc. prominent on one's name card. Formalities are more likely to be observed outside Budapest, but even within the capital some companies, such as banks, maintain more conservative cultures, and entry-level managers will obviously defer to senior officials in meetings.

SOCIAL FRAGMENTATION

That total Communist control caused society to fragment into tiny units that gained huge significance for the people they comprised. Ties of family and friendship, old classmates and teachers, neighbors and acquaintances became the stuff of society, because the normal tiers of civil society found in Western countries had been destroyed. Dependence on personal ties has remained in the post-Communist era since 1990. How this affects foreigners is discussed in Chapters 4 and 8.

Another legacy of the Communist period is the low inclination to save money. For all its faults, the

Communist system provided a welfare state (on huge foreign loans!): free medical care (although with brown paper envelopes often exchanging hands for "better service"); pensions based on right, not lifetime contributions; sick pay; the right to work; child care allowances; and subsidized cafeteria meals, food, clothing, housing, education, transportation, theater, books, recordings, and vacations, for example. Wages, on the other hand, were meager and showed little differentiation according to effort.

Productivity was low, and the heavy welfare spending was poorly matched with needs. Take public housing as an example. It was allocated according to a composite of criteria, of which "need" was only one. Often apartments were allocated to friends and relations of people with influence in the housing department.

Effectively, there was discrimination against the proletariat in what was supposed to be a proletarian state. Officials, clerical workers, and supervisors—hard to describe as working class—had a good chance of being allocated an apartment, but lower-ranking workers received, if they were lucky, a cheap plot of land on which to build a home in their spare time. The luckier, better-placed Party comrades had not only obtained some scarce public housing ready-made, but they paid very low rent for it.

Here was a situation of chronic housing shortage, with a great deal of government money being spent on subsidizing the rents of some of the people who least needed it. (Bizarrely, the same accusation is made today against the Orbán government, whose policies on tax, housing aid, and family support undoubtedly favor the middle and upper-classes over the less well off.)

SPENDING

There was little incentive to save in those days. Often the problem was to find something sensible to buy with the money you had. Many people did better by throwing parties for the rich and influential than they would have done by putting their money in the bank, as bank deposits shrank before one's eyes, earning negative real interest. Others built themselves marble bathrooms or enjoyed vacations abroad—Hungary, unlike most Soviet-bloc countries, allowed foreign travel to many citizens after 1964.

The high inflation of the 1990s did nothing to persuade people to be thrifty. Even today, the first investment choice for most families is property—spending on the home, a second home, a child's home, or a grandmother's home that will be inherited one day.

However, after the twin disasters of the foreign-exchange mortgages and global financial downturn of 2008 hit, there is evidence that some Hungarians are stashing away something for the future—even if some is via an Austrian savings account, chosen by many citizens in 2012 for the perceived extra security.

PATRIOTISM

Hungarians have a strong sense of nationhood. But this loyalty to the "nation" means two or even three things at once. Hungarians are loyal to their country and fellow citizens, regardless of social or ethnic affiliation. In other words, they are patriotic, rather in the way that Americans are patriotic. There is no British-style embarrassment about flying the flag or standing up to sing the stirring, haunting national anthem, "God Bless the Hungarians" (*Isten, áldd-meg a' Magyart*, written by Ferenc Kölcsey in 1823).

Hungarians identify with their linguistic community: the thirteen or fourteen million people in Hungary, Romania, Slovakia, Ukraine, Serbia, Croatia, Slovenia, and Austria whose native language is Hungarian. Most live in areas that belonged to the Kingdom of Hungary before the First World War.

Some people go on to identify a Hungarian cultural or even ethnic community to which they belong, and draw unsavory sociopolitical conclusions from that. The nation in this sense is seen as something positive, but monolithic, burdened, not enriched by its minorities or possessors of parallel identities. Most of the small linguistic minorities of present-day Hungary (Germans, Romanians, Slovaks, and other Slavs) have effectively been assimilated. The issue is seen at its most acute in relation to the Roma communities.

ATTITUDES TOWARD THE ROMA

Hungary is home to around 750,000 Roma— 7.5 percent of the population—according to the Budapest-based European Roma Rights Center— although the figures are only an estimate, since some Roma are reluctant to discuss their ethnicity in response to widespread racial prejudice. (The term *cigány*, the Hungarian for Gypsy, is coming to be seen as derogatory. The "weasel word" is *kisebbségi*— minority.)

Roma can usually be distinguished from other Hungarians. They tend to have darker skin, and their accents, clothes, customs, and body language are distinctive, at least to other Hungarians.

The highest proportions of Roma (some 10–12 percent of the population) are found in the relatively deprived northeast of the country and in Budapest. There are three subdivisions of the Roma: the "Hungarian" or "musical" Roma (all Hungarian speaking, the most integrated of the three), the Wallachian Roma (who may speak a Romany language known to linguists as Vlach Lovar), and the Beás Roma (who may still speak an archaic dialect of Romanian). While all Roma speak Hungarian, for about 17 percent it is a second language.

"The Roma are the real losers by the change of system," as Gábor Kertesi, a Hungarian authority, writes at the beginning of his study of Roma employment and education: "They lost their traditional crafts and economic functions in the first half of the twentieth century, and now they have lost the unskilled jobs in metal-bashing industries that they gained during the acute labor shortages of the Communist period."

While the situation of Hungarian Roma is not the worst in the region, it still shocking, with social disadvantage appearing in their social structure, employment, skills, education, housing, and state of health. Many live on the edge of villages with very poor, if not non-existent, amenities. An estimated 30 percent of working-age Roma are unemployed, but in the remoter provinces, the number is more likely to be around 90 percent. In some cases public works projects have improved the statistics. Many, especially the women, do casual work on a regular basis, particularly in agriculture.

Roma are far behind the general population in the amount of schooling they manage to complete. Only 19 percent of Hungarian Roma have completed secondary education, as against 69 percent of the general population. Non-governmental organizations supporting Roma repeatedly accuse local authorities of supporting segregated education in practice, although this is against the law.

Despite significant funding from the European Union for projects to help combat poverty, little lasting progress has been made. According to Tibor Derdák, a leader with a Buddhist movement running a school for Roma in Borsod county, northeast Hungary, much of the funding was wasted or diverted for private gain. He describes how one well-functioning school project in the town of Ózd was closed by a local authority immediately the contract guaranteed by EU funding ceased to apply. The school building, renovated with Union funds, was converted to a hotel by a local businessman and attempts made to continue the school work were blocked by the administrative pressure. (The hotel was a commercial failure, and soon closed.)

In Derdák's view, cynicism and prejudice prevail among provincial local authorities. "I don't know of any mayor who would speak about long-term programs for improving the situation of Roma youngsters. I have never heard of any such mayor, because they are convinced that they would never be reelected if they spoke about improving conditions for Gypsies," he says.

In May, 2016, the European Commission launched infringement proceedings against Hungary for persistent segregation of Roma in education (noting it has similar concerns regarding the situation in nearby Slovakia and Czech Republic).

The social facts leave the majority of Hungary's Roma as an underclass making little progress toward integration into the majority society or its economy.

ATTITUDES TOWARD AUTHORITY

Hungarians, by and large, are keen on law and order, but they haven't had entirely positive experiences with those who are supposed to keep it. At least not in the last ninety years or so.

Police, the secret services, and the Communist militia (now abolished) all came under the Ministry of the Interior in the Communist period and formed a state within a state, especially the network of informers in all walks of life and the agents controlling them. Their crimes are presented graphically at the House of Terror (Terror Háza, VI. Andrássy út 60.)

Ironically, a quarter of a century after the fall of Communism, critics of the Orbán government are uneasy about the expansion of various security forces created since 2010, purportedly to aid the "fight against terror," especially since Hungary has not experienced a serious terror attack since the early 1990s and is not seen as a prime target for Islamist militants.

Military conscription was abolished on November 3, 2004, when the last batch of Hungarians ended their compulsory military service. The move to professional armed forces brought Hungary into line with almost all EU countries.

MEN AND WOMEN

Although younger Hungarians follow more modern European trends toward equality between the sexes, relations between men and women in Hungary may still strike people from English-speaking countries as old-fashioned. Most couples seem to divide their responsibilities in a traditional way. Women cook, shop, and clean, while men look after money matters and the DIY, and do outdoor tasks such as mowing, digging, or car washing. Men may have become more involved in child rearing in recent decades but, as in the rest of Europe, there are fewer children to rear.

The courtesies due to women are obvious and the feminism of Hungarian women seldom extends to resenting these. A woman goes out of a room or into an elevator first. The man usually drives, pushes the stroller, and carries the bags. In the street, the man traditionally walks on the woman's left—apparently because of how swords were worn. Women are served before men in a restaurant. The bill is brought to the man, and the woman is helped on with her coat.

Even in the workplace, many of these courtesies are still observed. It's customary to compliment a woman on a new hairdo, and on her clothes from time to time. On the darker side, flirtation bordering on harassment can occur with young women at work, illustrated in recent years by the emergence of some high-profile cases of rape and sexual assault involving men misusing their senior positions.

FATHERS AND LOVERS

Hungarian men are demonstrative suitors, and to hear them talk, and watch them bow, smirk, and present bunches of flowers, you'd think you were in France or Italy. They also like to talk about their conquests; but before you lock up your daughters and threaten your spouse, consider whether they might not be exaggerating in this respect. A few reasons follow.

Extramarital relationships cost time and money, and few Hungarians have much of either.

Social life is centered on a circle of extended family and old friends. Hungarians do less business travel and have less time for fishing trips than their counterparts in English-speaking countries, making peccadilloes harder to hide.

Hungarians go to bed early. If, as the Hungarian writer George Mikes remarked in *How to Be an Alien*, "Continental people have sex life; the English have hot-water bottles," the Hungarians have second jobs, weight problems, a tendency to fall asleep in front of the television, children to attend to, nosy parents and siblings, politics to argue about, gardens to tend . . .

Although the divorce rate is high—at around 55 percent of all marriages—the cause is as likely to be estrangement, unacceptable behavior, violence, or drinking as infidelity. Even in cases of infidelity, spouses are likely to turn a blind eye or patch up their differences. Separation and divorce are expensive.

CHURCHGOING

According to the 2011 census, 37 percent of Hungarians are Roman Catholic (and another 1.8 percent Greek Catholic), 11.5 percent Calvinist, 2.2 percent Evangelical (Lutheran), and 0.1 percent religious Jews. However, while 16.6 percent said they have no religious affiliation, some 27 percent declined to answer the question on Church affiliation, and a mere 1.5 percent declared themselves atheist. Hence these statistics are only a guide to religious affiliation.

The figures for Hungary cast doubt on how far the religious decline can be blamed on the Communist regime as such, as they are in line with the tendencies in much of Europe.

There appear to be no reliable statistics on those attending church, with various surveys quoting numbers between 12 and 22 percent of the population. The latter figure seems too high, but certainly the

Orbán government has been eager to give the traditional Churches more power, and the increasing influence of Churches in education has resulted in anecdotal evidence of parents attending church in the hope of getting children accepted at the better schools.

Despite the fact that the dominant Catholic Church outlaws contraception, not to mention abortion and divorce, the birthrate is 9.3 per thousand, having bottomed out at 8.8 in 2011. There are some 32,000 abortions a year, down from a peak of 90,000 in 1990. Hungary has a high rate of divorce: in 2013 there were 20,200 divorces against almost 37,000 marriages.

Christian teaching was repressed in the Stalinist period of Communist rule, while official doctrines of atheistic materialism and supremacy of the state over the individual were taught in schools. Religious affiliations were incompatible with Communist Party membership, so churchgoers were in practice excluded from almost all positions of responsibility.

Toleration increased in the 1960s, but it came with stronger attempts to rope the Churches in to the political fabric, through Communist-run front organizations. The Churches were still tightly controlled by the State Office for Church Affairs and infiltrated by secret police and by fellow travelers—religious apologists for Communism. Attempts were made to pass on to the Catholic hierarchy the task of "controlling" the Church and ensuring that it served Communist political purposes.

Yet, despite the duplicitous nature behind the original policies, by the early 1980s religious toleration, at least by Communist standards, was highly advanced: for example, conscientious objectors from the Jehovah's Witnesses who refused military service could perform social or medical work—a system similar to the practice in West Germany at the time, but a rare privilege for a Warsaw Pact country.

Indeed, one of the very last pieces of legislation passed under the final, reform Communist government of 1989–90 was a new, surprisingly liberal law on recognition of Churches. The new environment led to a revival of religious activity, including the return of traditional Catholic religious orders, an influx of charismatic movements and nonconformist Churches such as the Mormons and Jehovah's Witnesses, and the establishment of non-Christian religious communities, including Hare Krishna, Buddhist, Muslim, and Bahá'í.

But societal conditions were far less favorable in 1990 than they had been in 1945. Two generations had grown up with little or no religious instruction. Although the Churches moved quickly to expand religious education of children, they found it hard to retain new adult members, whose churchgoing slackened off once the euphoria caused by the end of Communism was over.

The Orbán government, however, has its own ideas about religion, being been keen to support the so-called "historical" faiths, and most especially the Roman Catholic Church. At the same time, it has, in effect, discriminated against newer congregations. It claimed—without identifying a single example—that many religious organizations founded after 1990 were so-called "business Churches," that is, set up to take advantage of the lenient tax laws applicable to religious orders. On this tenuous basis, it controversially disenfranchised all but about thirty Churches and denominations deemed acceptable to the lawmakers. Although the government insists any religious group may worship according to its wishes, the law puts the "de-listed" denominations at a significant disadvantage financially and socially vis-à-vis the recognized groups.

ATTITUDES TOWARD SEXUAL MINORITIES

Hungary is among the most tolerant countries toward Lesbian, Gay, Bisexual, and Transgender people in Central Europe, and (on paper) the one with the best legal protection. Same-sex partnerships have been recognized since 1996; a registered partnership granting same-sex couples rights similar to those of spouses has been in place since 2009. However, same-sex marriage is not legal.

In spite of the relatively favorable legal situation, LGBTQI still face prejudice and discrimination in many areas of life and, as a result, most keep their sexual orientation and gender identity secret.

"Nearly every second Hungarian agrees with the statement that homosexuality is a sickness, and would rather not have a gay or lesbian neighbor," gay rights NGO Háttér notes on its Web site, http://en.hatter.hu/

In recent years, however, the atmosphere has become far less tense, although a significant police presence is always evident at the annual gay pride parade in Budapest.

chapter three

CUSTOMS & TRADITIONS

HIGH DAYS AND HOLIDAYS

Hungarians love vacations and make the most of them. Not just their summer breaks, but public holidays as well. The main ones are given below. It is important to make a note of public holidays or you may well turn up at the office and find nobody else there. (It has happened.) Whenever possible, working days are officially shifted to make a long weekend.

Holiday Dates

January 1 New Year's Day (újév)

March 15 Outbreak of the 1848 Revolution and national day (nemzeti ünnep)

(Movable) Good Friday (nagy péntek) at the time of publication is a proposed holiday, Easter Monday

May 1 Feast of Labor (a munka ünnepe) and anniversary of Hungary's entry into the EU

(Movable) Whitsun/Pentecost (pünkösd)

August 20 Foundation of the state, feast of St. Stephen of Hungary, and a national/state day (nemzeti és állami ünnep)

October 23 Anniversary of the outbreak of the 1956 Revolution and a national day (nemzeti ünnep)

November 1 All Saints' Day (mindenszentek napja)

December 24–26 Christmas (karácsony)

Several other days feature on the calendar of most families, including other Christian and Jewish holidays such as Ash Wednesday, Good Friday, Passover, Yom Kippur, All Souls' Day (halottak napja, November 2), Hanukkah, Christmas Eve (usually known as szenteste, or Holy Eve, December 24), and New Year's Eve (szilveszter, December 31). Religious families may also observe Lent and Advent in various ways. Carnival (farsang), between Epiphany (vízkereszt, January 6) and Ash Wednesday, the first day of Lent, is the traditional period for balls and other winter festivities. Villages sometimes hold a fair (búcsú) on or near the dedication feast of the parish church.

The southern town of Mohács comes alive on the last weekend before Lent, with a festival known as the busójárás. Folk music, craft fairs, and processions culminate on the Sunday with a parade of busó— mischievous men in heavy sheepskin coats and elaborate traditional wooden masks with horns. Schoolchildren observe April Fool's Day (bolondok napja, April 1) and are often given a chance to teach their teachers on that day. By the Danube in Budapest is one good place to be on August 20, for a morning regatta and a lavish evening fireworks display.

Halloween, on October 31, is an occasion for young people to party by wearing masks or fancy dress.

Almost all Hungarians visit family graves on All Saints' Day to leave flowers and candles. If they can't make it on November 1 they'll go the next day or on the closest weekend.

The main anniversaries celebrate the outbreak of the 1848 Revolution (March 15), the foundation of the State (August 20), and the 1956 Revolution (October 23), but other historical commemorations may include the liberation of Hungary from German troops in 1944 (around April 4), the signing of the 1920 Treaty of Trianon (June 4), the withdrawal of the last Soviet occupation troops in 1991 (June 30), the execution of the 1849 martyrs of Arad (October 6), and the reoccupation of Budapest by Soviet forces in 1956 (November 4).

FAMILY OCCASIONS
Christmas (Karácsony)

Hungarians celebrate Christmas in much the same way as people in English-speaking countries, but the timing is different. Children traditionally clean their boots on December 5 and leave one or both of them between the leaves of a double window overnight. St. Nicholas (Mikulás, Santa Claus) fills them, usually with sweets, nuts, and oranges. In theory, only good children receive presents; bad children are supposed to get a beating instead, from Krampusz, a devil figure dressed in black. The only Euro-compatible vestige of this is that a switch of gold-painted twigs is included in the Santa Claus booty. Kindergartens and schools often hold a Santa Claus celebration and may mark Christmas before they break up for the holiday.

The main festivities begin on Christmas Eve (szenteste). Shops close about midday and public transportation stops running by five o'clock. At home, the Christmas tree is decorated, and presents are placed around it. Catholic families often put a wooden Nativity group under the tree. A carol or two is sung before the presents

are opened. Then there is a family supper, which traditionally includes carp or other freshwater fish, and *bejgli*, a rich cake made of pastry and filled with ground walnuts or poppy seeds.

Christmas Eve is an intimate family occasion. Any visiting among neighbors ends by about 5:00 p.m. Catholic families attend midnight mass. The time for visiting or entertaining the extended family and friends is December 25 and 26 or later in the week, as few people seem to do much work between Christmas and New Year. Indeed, many private companies close down between the two holidays.

New Year's Eve (Szilveszter)
New Year's Eve is a more sociable occasion than Christmas. Most people celebrate among friends, in someone's home, in a restaurant, or in the street. It can be noisy, with fireworks and rattles. Main streets are closed to traffic, and public transportation in Budapest, for instance, is free. It's considered good luck to pull the tail of a piglet at New Year. Roast suckling pig is a traditional New Year's Eve dish. So are frankfurters after

midnight and lentils (good luck again) next morning
to banish your hangover.

Easter (Húsvét)

This is another big family occasion. The Easter meal on
Saturday, after sunset, consists of hard-boiled eggs and
ham with horseradish (grated, or grated and pickled),
and a braided milk loaf called *kalács*. Most children like
to stain or paint eggs for Easter Sunday breakfast. The
traditional stain is onionskin, but powdered dyes in
various colors are also used.

On Easter Monday, it's customary for boys and

men to sprinkle girls and women
they meet with a few drops of
cologne. They're rewarded for
this with an Easter egg (painted
or chocolate) and a peck on each
cheek. Most girls wash their hair
thoroughly on Easter Monday to
remove the smell of ill-chosen
cologne. Earlier customs were
much more exciting, with village
lads splashing buckets of well
water over the lasses—a folksy wet
T-shirt competition, dripping with
anthropological poignancy.

Other Special Days

Mother's Day (anyák napja) is kept on the first Sunday
in May, and Children's Day (gyereknap) on the last.
International Women's Day (nemzetközi nőnap, March
8) is also remembered to some extent, although it's felt
by some to have been a Communist invention. Father's
Day and Labor Day are not known, but May Day is
marked as a working-class festival, mainly by trade

unionists and left-wingers, often with a *majális*—a communal outdoor picnic with stands, sideshows, and speeches—rather than the kind of mass military parade customary in the Communist period.

Wine-growing communities hold elaborate vintage celebrations in the fall, and as many families own some vines, the grape harvest (*szüret*) and winemaking turn into other family occasions. So does pig slaughtering in November or December, at least in the country. Many hands are required to make all the traditional pork products (*disznótoros*) in a single day.

One more day worth noting: September 1, which is the usual starting day of the school year. Apart from having your kids ready, note that in Budapest and larger towns there is a huge increase in peak-hour traffic as parents feel they must drive their offspring to school. This surge falls away as pupils start to use public transportation.

NAME DAYS

Although birthdays are celebrated, at least for children, a person's fête or "name day" (*névnap*) is more important to the outside world. Family, friends, and colleagues should be greeted personally or called on their name day. Women often receive flowers and men a bottle of drink or something edible. Children receive presents from relations and school friends.

The first step to discovering when friends' and colleagues' name days are is to obtain a Hungarian calendar. However, several common names, such as Mária, István, and Erzsébet, have more than one name day, and it is worth checking which of these someone celebrates. There's an eight-day period of grace, within which you can still wish somebody a happy name day.

If your name is Kylie, or Brian, for that matter, you won't find your name in the Hungarian calendar. Bad luck! If you like, just select a similar Hungarian name for yourself and celebrate on the appropriate day.

FROM BIRTH TO DEATH

Hungarian babies have to be registered with the state within eight days. Most of them receive a single given name, but about 5 percent are given two.

The surname comes before the given name or names in Hungarian, but Hungarians prefer the international order when referring to themselves in other languages. So Kovács János becomes János Kovács in English. Some people have double-barreled surnames, which may be hyphenated or not. The practice of naming a boy after his father or godfather is common. The father is then referred to in writing as id. Kovács János (János Kovács Senior) and the son as ifj. Kovács János (János Kovács Junior).

Almost half the babies born in Hungary are baptized into the Catholic Church, sometimes receiving an additional baptismal name at that time. The ceremony may be followed by a party in a restaurant or at home. Most other denominations have similar ceremonies.

Catholic children take their first communion at a minimum age of eight and undergo confirmation (*bérmálás*) at the age of seventeen or eighteen, after attending religious instruction for several years beforehand. Confirmation into the Reformed and Evangelical (Lutheran) Churches usually comes at the age of about thirteen or fourteen. Jewish boys and girls have their bar or bat mitzvah at the age of thirteen and twelve respectively.

Hungarian weddings can be lavish, with several hundred people invited. The civil wedding takes place in a register office. About two-thirds of couples follow this with a religious ceremony of some kind. But in cities, not all those invited to the wedding ceremony are also invited to the reception. Those who are invited consult with the parents about what gift the couple would like. However, at a big traditional wedding, there will be a bride's dance: male guests asking the bride to dance place a

gift of money in a hat. Go on, be generous! Make it 10,000 forints (US $35). Foreign guests may need to practice the national dance, the csárdás, beforehand.

Funerals can also be big, but usually only the immediate family or chosen friends are invited back to the house or to a restaurant. Most funerals are held at cemetery chapels, where those arriving place their flowers on or around the coffin. After the service, the coffin is taken to the grave, with the mourners following. Cremation is common. It is customary for everyone to go over to the chief mourners and express condolences after the graveside prayers. Attendance at a funeral is an affirmation of intimacy with the bereaved family that is noted and appreciated (see page 72).

Traditionally, widows wore mourning for many months after the death of a husband, but this is observed only in villages these days.

chapter four

FRIENDS & MANNERS

Manners are closely connected with speech in Hungary, and so there are a good few Hungarian words in this chapter. Have a look at the pronunciation guide on page 158 if need be.

A SMILE FOR A SMILE

"The reply to a smile is a smile," as the Hungarian writer István Mácz points out. Hungary is not a closed society, just an atomized one, where personal friendship has added importance. Foreigners are welcomed and appreciated, but the approach is slightly different from that of Western Europe and North America. What social relations in Hungary are mainly about is exchanging the favors, affection, support, and assistance that help people to cope with a monolithic, anonymous, inimical outside world. Quite a responsibility, in fact.

Ties of kinship and friendship are the basis of honesty and trust in Hungary, with important implications for family life, social relations, and business. Many of the friendships go back a long way. Secondary-school classmates form a network that may help them for years. As for foreign friends, they're seen as an asset. For one thing, Hungarians are interested in how things are done abroad. For another, they want to present their country and society in a favorable light.

Often, foreigners in other countries have a feeling of being among people better educated than themselves, though many expatriates in Hungary possess the kind of expertise that post-Communist Hungarians still find valuable. But Hungary, like every country, has a stock of general knowledge appropriate to its society. Foreigners hoping to integrate into Hungarian society will have to pick up some of that general knowledge and look about them. Your considered judgments about Hungary—especially if favorable—will be music to the ears of your new Hungarian friends.

This is not to say that nothing can be criticized in Hungarian company. There are plenty of legitimate targets: the government, the tax system, the stores, drivers, the police, soccer managers, today's children, young people, the middle-aged, and the old. A good time will be had by all when tearing any of these to shreds. What remain sacrosanct are society itself and its fabric and customs—aspects of Hungary that can't reasonably be blamed on globalization, global warming, foreign intervention, or government stupidity. With these, tread softly, because you tread upon their dreams.

CONVERSATION AND CULTURE

Hungarians, educated or ill-educated, don't subscribe to the view increasingly found in Britain and the United States that all forms of culture are equivalent in value. They don't equate Maria Callas with Janis Joplin, as a BBC television series once did, even if they prefer the latter. They won't put television on a par with theater, or gardening with sculpture, or value Japanese cartoon techniques such as anime as highly as fine art. There's still a traditional pecking order in the arts—from "high" to "middle-brow" to "low." That's not to say that Hungarians won't be fascinated to hear foreigners' arguments on the other side. They're eager customers for Hollywood films, foreign rock, British comedy, Irish music, Scandinavian design, Chinese proverbs, and even Mexican soap operas.

Conversation in Hungary typically covers a much wider range of subjects than it does in a British living room or pub, or American family room or bar, as Hungarians sometimes find to their cost abroad. János Kornai, a celebrated economist, spoke for many when he recalled ruefully how, as a Harvard professor, "we once had three couples to our house, including two great economists and an equally famous political scientist . . . [but] the conversation was on conventional subjects."

Which is more natural, chitchat or discourse? Leaving your work, studies, politics, artistic sensibilities, religion, and *Weltanschauung* behind before you set out to see your friends, and talking about baseball, car maintenance, babies, recipes, and knitting patterns instead? Or walking in and sitting down to weigh the affairs of the world or anything else that springs to mind during the conversation?

Mind you, conversation Hungarian-style is not an art learned overnight. Be careful to keep a light touch, to avoid direct contradiction, or at least phrase it in question form. Remember to show interest and respect for ideas you disagree with, and if everyone is speaking English resist the temptation to use your linguistic advantage to impose your own.

One reason, in fact, why Hungarians make witty, entertaining conversationalists is their background in the Communist system, which told you what to think and provided endless, rather facile reasons. The often circular, quibbling, specious arguments of the authorities honed people's conversational skills, turning oppression into a source of mirth. Since then, the post-Communist period and the side effects of democracy, capitalism, privatization, and globalization have provided equally inspiring subjects of discourse. But, be wary, unless you are very confident of your company, of offering opinion on the hottest subject of all—current local politics. The subject, always divisive, has become acutely so since 2010. Of course, you can listen, by all means, whatever the political color of your hosts. Enjoy your meal!

MAKING FRIENDS

Hungarians attach great importance to friendship and file people mentally as friends, relations, or acquaintances. Friendships are long-term and have important functions in society and the economy.

There's a freemasonry among foreigners in Budapest, and "old Hungary hands" can often help you to make contact with Hungarian society as well. Budapest and several provincial towns have clubs and institutions where foreigners can meet, including national chambers of

commerce and an international women's club, for instance. There are Web sites, online chat groups, and still two English-language newspapers that give plenty of clues as to where to find other foreigners.

Friendship for Hungarians includes effort. You put yourself out for your friends and expect them to do the same for you, even after a couple of years' gap. Hungarians are big on the symbolic value of actions, so that a small, unexpected gift or a helping hand can provide the opening to friendship. They like to rely on their friends. Early progress toward friendship may be lost by being momentarily offhand. Hungarians also need to be given opportunities to show friendship toward you. Don't shy away from imposing on them in small ways, or accepting small favors.

LANGUAGE PROBLEMS

When it comes to making friends with Hungarians, there is often a formidable language barrier with the over-forties, who may well not have learned any English in school. And even those who have done so may be shy and unwilling to put themselves forward, particularly in front of native speakers. Although many young, educated Hungarians are outstanding in English, and sometimes German and Russian, a study published in 2011 by Eurostat revealed 63 percent of Hungarian adults had no knowledge of a foreign language, a result that compares badly with nearby countries —in Poland, for example, the figure was 38 percent and in Slovenia a mere 7.6 percent.

English is entirely different from Hungarian, both in vocabulary and concept, which makes the task of learning English more formidable for Hungarians than for most other Europeans. And there are other barriers.

One is shared with the British and Americans—the absence of a language-learning culture. Outside the intellectual elites, few children grow up with the example of a good foreign-language speaker in the family, partly because Russian, the compulsory language in schools from the 1940s to the 1980s, was scorned for political reasons. And all foreign-language films are dubbed into Hungarian. This means that even those who have studied English in school may struggle to understand native speakers. Foreigners in mixed Hungarian and foreign company must expect quite a lot of Hungarian to be spoken around them.

That, of course, is one spur to learning the Hungarian language. There'll be plenty of encouragement from locals, who will be delighted with even the slightest knowledge you may display.

"Every language is unique, the Hungarian language is even more unique," writes Ágnes Nemes Nagy, introducing a selection of her work translated into English, and a few lines later, "All poetry is untranslatable, Hungarian poetry is even more untranslatable." Surely English is unique too, isn't it, and quite untranslatable? Arguably, yes. Furthermore, Hungarian contains far more loan words from other languages—Latin, German, French, English, Turkish, and (especially) Slavic tongues—than native speakers generally realize. Still, Nemes Nagy's remark is interesting as an example of the affection and pride in which Hungarians hold their language.

Be that as it may, while it may appear impossible at first sight, everyday Hungarian is no more difficult or time-consuming to learn than most other foreign languages. Look on the bright side. The Roman alphabet is used. Hungarian employs few sounds that can't, at least with practice, be pronounced reasonably well by English-speakers (for more on this, see pages 157–58). Spelling is largely phonetic, and the structure of an inflected language like Hungarian is easy to pin down because its rules can neatly be captured in tables and other visual aids.

BEHAVIOR

Good manners begin with a greeting. Stand up! Only the old and frail stay seated for greetings. The practice in Hungary is for a man to make the first greeting to a woman, a younger person to an older, a subordinate to a superior, a salesperson to a customer, and someone entering or approaching to those already present. It's bad manners not to greet people, and worse not to return a greeting.

Having begun the chapter with smiles, it should be said at this point that Hungarians don't usually smile at strangers because it seems too familiar. Americans in particular are startled by the somber expressions they may meet with in Hungarian stores and restaurants, misinterpreting them as rudeness or indifference. But go into a store or restaurant a second time, and there's likely to be a nod or even a smile to accompany the greeting.

People meeting for the first time give a formal handshake and exchange names. They may also mutter "*Örvendek*" ("Delighted"). There's no need for a third party to effect an introduction. A card is worth offering if you have one, as it's hard for both sides to catch foreign names the first time around.

It's customary to shake hands with everyone, known or unknown, if you're entering a meeting or group. Men or women kiss women on each cheek if they know them socially, and even at work, but only silver-haired roués kiss a woman's hand these days. Today there's no need for men to click their heels as they bow, impressive though this looks in pre-war Hungarian movies. Male relatives may kiss each other, but this won't be expected of foreigners. Even teenagers among themselves observe some of these customs. Adults should include older children in greetings rituals, unless they're obviously hanging back. Foreign children should be encouraged to join in, too.

A plain greeting (no handshake) is also given to strangers as you enter or leave an elevator or a railway compartment, but not a bus or a streetcar. If you have to share a table in a restaurant or cafeteria, the correct greetings are "*Jó étvágyat!*" "(Bon appetit!) to those already eating when you arrive, "*További jó étvágyat!*"("Further bon appetit!") to those still at it when you stand up to go, and "*Egészségére!*" ("To your health!") to people finishing their meal.

LOST FOR WORDS

The problem for Hungarians meeting foreigners is that many of the nuances of behavior vanish if Hungarian is not being spoken. This leaves them uncomfortable about how to behave. The degrees of familiarity in Hungarian range from using the second person (like *tu* in French) to relations, friends, children, or animals, to the third person with the name of the person addressed, or a pronoun (there are two, one more formal than the other).

Hungarians who speak good English may know that they should address strangers as Mr. or Mrs., but it goes against the grain with them to do so, because the equivalent forms in Hungarian are not particularly polite.

Nine times out of ten, Hungarians who are acquainted call each other by their given names, and express familiarity or politeness simply by their use of the second or third person. When the name is not known, or if extra politeness of address is required, a Hungarian might say, "*Mérnök úr*" ("Mr. Engineer"), "*Szomszéd úr*" ("Mr. Neighbor"), *Tanárnő* ("Ms. Teacher"), or *Igazgató asszony* ("Mrs. Manager"). None of these forms translates well into English, which can leave Hungarians lost for words. Foreigners should quickly put people out of their misery by suggesting their given name, as in, "Please call me Jack," and asking, "What can I call you?"

The problem is compounded with married women. In many cases, they take their husband's full name when they marry. For example, on marrying János Kovács (Kovács János in Hungarian), Gabriella Takács becomes Kovács Jánosné, and "Gabriella" doesn't even feature in her ID! Well, that has to be translated as Mrs. János Kovács. The alternatives open to brides these days are Gabriella Kovács (Kovács Gabriella) or not changing her name at all (quite common).

FORMS OF ADDRESS

Hungarian greetings and forms of address are worth learning. Taking the polite forms first, *Csókolom* (an abbreviation of "I kiss your hand") is used when meeting and saying good-bye, by men to women, and by children to grown-ups. Otherwise the usual greetings between strangers or those on formal terms would be *Jó reggelt kívánok* ("Good morning") early in the morning, *Jó napot kívánok* ("Good day") until early evening, *Jó estét kívánok* ("Good evening") thereafter, and *Jó éjszakát* ("Good night") if someone's off to bed.

Another fairly formal greeting between acquaintances is *Üdvözlöm* ("I greet you"). The commonest farewell is *Viszontlátásra* ("Till we see each other again").

The familiar form of address—known as *tegezés*, from *te*, the Hungarian second person singular pronoun—is indicated by its use in a verb, and is used to and among children and young adults, between women of a similar age, relations, and familiar friends after they have specifically agreed to do so.

Normally a suggestion of being on familiar terms would come from a woman to a man, or an older person to a younger. Some less well-educated Hungarians appear to think that foreigners are children because they can't speak Hungarian properly, and accordingly go for *tegezés*. This should usually be gracefully accepted. However, *tegezés* is the form for insults as well. Lip-readers testify that car drivers always use the familiar forms when suggesting how pedestrians or other drivers should behave.

It's impolite to return the wrong greeting—either to adopt familiarity unasked or to spurn familiarity proffered by others, unless you can somehow imply that you're not worthy of the honor. Foreigners who accidentally use a familiar form in addressing someone may find that the Hungarian instantly understands and accepts it, with no harm done, but it's not an elegant mistake!

Another point: being on familiar terms with one of a married couple doesn't automatically mean you're on familiar terms with the other, let alone their grown-up children. *Tegezés* between adults is symmetrical, so that if older people use it to people much younger than themselves, aside from very young children, they may put the younger person in a spot. The last thing the young want is to seem familiar to Daddy's business partner, for instance. They may even get the unfortunate impression that they're being treated like a child.

What forms of address are used at work will depend on the boss. It would be odd if those of the same sex who were involved in a common project— say on an informal committee—didn't go for *tegezés*. The same would apply to people helping each other to build a house, kill a pig, make a patchwork quilt, or mend a motorcycle.

NODS AND BOWS

Being on familiar terms may imply frankness, friendship, or identity of aims, but it doesn't necessarily imply equality, so if you address your boss in the familiar form, as requested, a little extra politeness may still be in order. A nod or a slight bow, or introducing what you have to say with a formula such as, "excuse me for disturbing you," will make the boss think what a well-mannered person this new young foreigner is, and what a pleasure it is to have him or her in the firm.

One way to sidestep these problems, you might think, is to stick to English, but it doesn't really resolve them, because it leaves your relationships awkwardly undefined in terms of degree of politeness, at least for Hungarians. So greeting people in Hungarian is a good habit to cultivate. It also gives you useful information about how they feel about their relationship with you. Stammering out a "*Jó napot kívánok*" (formal), and getting a smile and an emphatic "*Szervusz*" (familiar) in reply, means that you can be a bit more friendly than you thought.

Hello and Good-bye

Most of the many, many familiar words for hello in Hungarian also mean good-bye. The commonest hail or farewell between adults on familiar terms is *szervusz*, derived from the Latin *servus*, servant. Alternatives are *szia, szevasz,* and *szerbusz*. In fact *szia* and, increasingly, *helló*, are probably the commonest familiar greetings heard today. (Just don't address the elderly lady next door with the same greeting. It might be so inappropriate as to be comical to others—but it might induce a heart attack for its rudeness to the dear herself.)

That's only the tip of the iceberg. Young or earnestly cool people use endless, sometimes short-lived, alternatives—*szeva, szió, szióka, sziamia,* and *sziómió* come from *szervusz*. *Helló* (even on departure), *hellóka, helóbeló, hahó, holi,* and *holihó* form another group, but it's worth noting that *hallo* means something different: it's used for calling someone across a field or a telephone line.

Csáo, csá, csácsumi, csákány, cső, csocsesz, csocsi, csovi, csőváz, and *csumi* are among the commoner *ciao* derivatives. *Puszi, pusszancs,* and similar words simply mean a peck on the cheek. A truncated *pá* ("bye") is used by elderly ladies as a farewell.

Hungarian is flexible—just follow suit!

Actually, the smart way to say good-bye in Hungarian is to use a phrase appropriate to the situation. Just a few of the many: *Jó pihenést* ("Have a good rest," said to people leaving work), *Jó munkát* ("Good work"), *Jó mulatást* ("Have fun"), *Jó kirándulást* ("Good trip").

Children may address men as "X *bácsi*" and women as "X *néni*" (the equivalent to "Uncle X" and "Auntie X" respectively, in English). Adults do the same to people twenty or more years older than themselves, even if they are on familiar second-person terms. This should be avoided with ladies of a certain age who have taken great care with their appearance, or still play tennis in a geriatric sort of way. Men can have the extra-polite formula "X *bátyám*" up their sleeve for very eminent men with whom they're on familiar terms—your wife's godfather, or an elderly high-court judge, say.

The point of all this is the usefulness of taking some Hungarian lessons if you're going to be living in Hungary for a while. Even if you speak English with your friends and colleagues, a good Hungarian teacher is an invaluable source of information on how to behave politely. A teacher, by the way, is addressed as *Tanár úr* if male and *Tanárnő* if female, with plenty of earnest nods and not too many have-a-good-day smiles, unless known very well. Actors, artists, musicians, opera singers, ballet dancers, contortionists, and trapeze artists are addressed as *Művész úr* or *Művésznő*.

INVITATIONS HOME

An invitation to the home is, of course, a personal honor. If it's from a business partner, it may be wise to dress up, but as often as not it can be quite informal (if unsure, ask). It's the norm to bring flowers for the lady of the house, and/or a bottle of wine. If children are involved, some small presents are appropiate.

Although it is no longer *de rigueur*, it may be the house style to remove your shoes in the hall. Best to offer, and ask for slippers, especially in winter. A long, hearty and delicious meal is likely to be served, so go easy on the tid-bits that are offered beforehand.

Hungarians like books, and your hosts are likely to boast many shelves of literary volumes. Even if they are rarely read these days, they make for good topics of conversation. Anything from urban architecture to child care, psychology to wildlife on the puszta. Most Hungarians are besotted with history, but, unless you are prepared to listen, that might be contentious, since "recent" means anything from the eighteenth century onward. Be aware that—along with the heavy defeats and suffering incurred from fighting against Soviet forces—bombers from both the USAF and the RAF raided Hungary in 1944-45, and many Hungarians consider that the USA encouraged, then failed the country in the 1956 Uprising.

History also invariably leads to current politics. That, of course, is the most contentious of all subjects. Steer clear, unless you are prepared for a lecture: offer counter opinions only at your peril.

HUNGARIANS AT HOME

HOUSE AND HOME

While much renovation work has been done in the past two decades, many visitors to Hungary are struck by the poor condition of residential buildings. Certainly, the shabby apartment blocks in cities and tumbledown houses in villages make a sharp contrast with neighboring Austria, for example. But however scruffy the block may look, step into a Budapest apartment and you're likely to enter a spotless, well-decorated, and comfortable home. Hungarian housewives spend more time on their homes than their counterparts in any other nation in Europe.

The poor maintenance of buildings applies especially to the apartment blocks, which in most cases were sold by the state to tenants at rock-bottom prices in the early 1990s. Owners have since found it difficult to reach agreement among themselves on maintenance costs or to chase down those who neglect to pay. Maintenance charges often remain low, as a glance at halls, stairways, and elevators shows. This applies equally to fine late-nineteenth-century houses and to the 1960s and '70s prefabricated tower blocks (so-called "*panel ház*" in Hungarian).

Most Hungarians live in what people in English-speaking countries would class as cramped conditions: while there is a trend to larger homes, a typical apartment of 700 square feet (65 sq. m) will often house a family of three or four. A room may often serve two or more purposes—such as a living room and study by day, and a bedroom by night. Almost 40 percent of dwellings in Hungary are apartments.

Wholesale privatization of housing in the 1990s has left about 90 percent of homes owned privately and 10 percent publicly owned. This is similar to Germany (6 percent), but much lower than the proportion of "social rented housing" in the UK. Although tenants were able to buy their homes cheaply, they were not prepared for the true cost of running them. Despite local authority grants made available to assist renovation, a significant minority of the new condominiums are in financial straits.

The easy money available from 2004 to 2008 resulted in 35,000–40,000 new homes being built each year. The economic downturn induced a slump in the building trade, with just 7,300 built in 2013. Sector experts expect government measures to boost numbers to around 11,000 in 2016.

Much of central Budapest consists of traditional, six-story, late-nineteenth-century apartment blocks. The typical block is built around one or more

courtyards, with a grand staircase on the street side and access to the apartments along open corridors running around on each floor.

Unlike similar blocks in most European countries, they were built for a broad social mix of tenants. The ground floor on the street side was given over to shops or workshops. The concierge (*házmester*) and his assistant (*vice*) lived modestly in dank, single-room dwellings at the back of the ground floor. The cheapest apartments were on the uppermost floors at the back, and the largest and most expensive, with the highest ceilings, were on the lower levels, on the street side of the block. A grand apartment consisted of up to six interconnecting rooms, a kitchen, a bathroom, and servants' quarters. Most of these large apartments were divided up after the Second World War, but some survive, and can be found for rent or sale.

THE DAILY ROUND

The average day typically begins early in Hungary. Although modern office life may still begin at 8:30 or even 9:00 a.m., school usually starts at 8:00 a.m., and this means the kids must usually be out of home by 7:30 a.m., possibly earlier if parents have to ferry them to different locations by car—an increasingly common phenomenon in Budapest, despite the good public transportation system.

Lunch is typically fairly light, with the main meal in the evening somewhere after 6:00 p.m. Non-working housewives may well use the day to shop for fresh food in the markets, but increasingly, with both parents working, dinners are getting simpler and are often delivered—the latter an unheard of service pre-1990.

If at school, the children are likely to get home only after 4:00 p.m., and be occupied with homework for much of the evening.

Time constraints have also impacted on shopping habits, and with spacious Western-style supermarkets in every city, the weekly family shop is typically done by car, or delivered to the door via an on-line order.

COST OF LIVING

Hungarians generally earn much less than Western Europeans and North Americans. The average gross monthly salary stood at Ft 265,000 (US $940, €850) in spring 2016. Naturally, many daily costs—public transportation, childcare, entertainment, and health care—are much lower than in Western Europe or North America. In addition, there are differences even within Hungary—the cost of living in Budapest and the western regions being higher than elsewhere.

Many compensate by working overtime or taking a second job, which cuts into their leisure time. That being said, the basic working week in most jobs is forty to forty-eight hours long, and employees have a good vacation entitlement of three to five weeks.

THE FAMILY

In most Hungarian families both the husband and the wife work outside the home. On average, men work longer hours than women, often taking a second job on the side, but women typically do most, if not all, of the housework and cooking.

Although three-generation households are becoming rare today in cities, quite a high proportion of Hungarian families involve grandparents in bringing up the children, certainly if they live nearby.

Children are watched and pampered in a way that parents in Western Europe or North America would find odd. Where parents are able, they follow their children's school studies very closely, often organizing extra tuition and helping them with homework.

Young teenagers in middle-class families attend organized activities on weekday afternoons—sports, extra lessons, music, and so on. This leaves them comparatively little time to develop the kind of youth subcultures found in Western Europe and North America. Their weekends are dominated by family chores, visits, and activities, although some take on "entrepreneurial" work, such as babysitting.

EDUCATION

Education, certainly for middle-class families, has burgeoned in the last two decades, even as the number of children has declined. Most parents like their children to have as much education as possible.

There are three tiers of education. Elementary schools normally provide eight grades of primary education. Then come three or four years of secondary education (although some secondary schools open their doors to a limited number of younger students). It is also mandatory for children aged three to attend kindergarten.

Teaching is far more formal than in schools in English-speaking countries. The *érettségi*, or graduation (school-leaving) certificate, is normally taken in four to seven subjects, including Hungarian, math, history, and a foreign language. Grades resulting from these exams, and from the last two years' schoolwork, are the basis for deciding who will be admitted to study what in higher education.

In the 2015–16 school year, some 524,000 pupils were receiving secondary education, of which around 40 percent attended general secondary schools (*gymnasia*—academically biased schools), 40 percent secondary vocational schools (*szakközépiskola*—somewhat akin to technical college level, which offer a form of *érettségi*) and 20 percent a vocational school (*szakiskola* and *speciális szakiskola*—trade level education, with no *érettségi*). As of 2014, 73 percent of eighteen-year olds were still in full-time education, down from a peak of 80 percent in 2010. In the nineteen–to–twenty-four age group, 23.4 percent were in full-time tertiary education.

Some *gymnasia* offer a year's intensive language learning before the ninth grade and then use two languages of instruction for the four-year secondary course. This means that most subjects, apart from Hungarian and history, are taught in the foreign language. There are fee-paying American, Austrian, British, German, French, Japanese, Chinese, and international schools in Budapest. (Nationals of some of these schools can attend free.)

There are a handful of private primary and secondary schools. Boarding schools in the British or American sense are hardly known, but students living far from their schools are given subsidized hostel (*kollégium*) accommodation nearby.

THE ORBÁN EDUCATIONAL "REFORMS"

Hungarians are especially proud of their
education system's achievements, but the
underlying philosophy, historically (and in line
with the regional traditions), emphasized factual
knowledge rather than critical thinking.

The Socialist–liberal coalitions between 2002
and 2010 pushed to introduce a system where the
students were encouraged to be self-motivated.
The school-leaving age was also raised to eighteen,
which meant students from disadvantaged
backgrounds, including Roma, were forced to
continue studies.

However, the Orbán government elected in
2010 immediately set about root and branch
changes in education. Billed as a reform package
necessary to cut waste and prepare Hungarian
youth for jobs in the modern economy, it cut
the number of funded university places, most
particularly in the arts and humanities, and
increased the role of secondary vocational schools
while reducing their academic input—all designed
to produce skilled blue-collar workers and
technicians suitable for the manufacturing "work-
based society" that the government sees as the
future for the economy.

At the primary and secondary level, the
government has both encouraged the traditional
Churches to take over schools—around 12 percent
of all primary and secondary schools are now
owned and run by Churches, against just 4 percent
in 2005—while nationalizing all other schools
formerly owned by local authorities. These are
under the close control of a central authority, the

Klebelsberg Institute (usually referred to by its Hungarian acronym, KLIK).

Whatever the potential long-term benefits, the changes have caused widespread protests in the teaching profession, even among government supporters. Critics accuse the government of destroying the already limited flexibility in the system and intentionally helping to stratify children into predictable "flows," meaning working-class kids will be channeled into blue-collar jobs, while only those from middle- and upper-class families will have access to the elite schools and universities.

For the underclass, including the Roma, reforms introduced in the runup to joining the European Union that raised the school-leaving age to eighteen have been abandoned, naturally resulting in a reduction of seventeen- and eighteen-year olds continuing their education.

SWEET SORROW

Students in their last year of high school have a busy time. As if the all-important final exams weren't enough, there are other matters to attend to.

First comes the Ribbon Inauguration Ball, usually in the fall, to which families are invited. Each graduate receives a ribbon with the years of attendance on it, and it's worn proudly in the lapel for the rest of the school year. Each final-year class has spent months preparing a display dance, often rather daring and modern. Then a quick change, and the teenagers dance a perfect Viennese waltz. A tableau is made with photographs of the classes and their teachers. This is usually displayed in a local shop.

Next comes the Parade in May. Classrooms and corridors are decorated with flowers. Graduates form a file, each with a hand on the shoulder in front, and shuffle through the whole school, laden with the flowers thrust upon them, singing "*Gaudeamus igitur*" and other traditional songs. The eleventh-graders give a little party bag to each graduate containing a forint coin to symbolize wealth, some salt to work up a thirst for knowledge, and a savory scone for their journey into the wide world.

Between the end of the Parade and the end of the exams, graduates may visit the teachers at home, serenading them from the street, then enjoying an evening of reminiscing. Finally comes a restaurant banquet, and arrangements are made for everyone to meet up in one, five, ten, twenty, and fifty years' time.

One fairly recent add-on to all these events, especially popular in Budapest, is the so-called "after party" (hip teenagers use the English words), arranged at night after the official Ball, when the otherwise civilized and well-behaved young ladies and gentlemen usually consume vast amounts of alcohol. As one Budapest parent of two teenagers put it: "The event usually lasts until the early hours of the next day, and what typically follows is a two-day hangover on the school leavers' part. If your class/school does not organize an After after the Ball, you are simply not "*menő*," you are not cool, so it is a must-do event."

LOVE AND SEXUALITY
Love and sexuality are eagerly and frankly discussed in Hungary, but generally attitudes are more conservative than in Western Europe. This applies especially to the young and those who look after them.

The age of consent for sexual activity between persons of different sexes is fourteen. Hungarians may marry at eighteen, or at sixteen with permission from a parent or guardian. The age of consent for homosexual activity is also eighteen, and this is the lower legal age limit for "sex workers."

However, for more conservative or religious families, girls are normally seen as off-limits to their peers and to adults until they finish school at about eighteen. Such families may try to stop relationships developing between teenagers, in case they "get out of hand" or interfere with schoolwork.

Although almost all schools are mixed, boys and girls don't reintegrate fully until their mid-teens.

More liberal parents, aware that opportunities for sexual relationships to develop can always be found or created, try to get to know boyfriends, invite them round and even to sleep over in later high school years.

Firm figures on teenage sexual activity are hard to come by. Certainly teenage pregnancies have plummeted: in 1980, there were 68 live births per thousand women aged fifteen to nineteen. This had fallen to 40 by 1990, and then halved to 20 by 2003, a rate roughly maintained ever since. Many of these young mothers have had only eight, or fewer, years of formal education.

Naturally, this trend may be the result of increased use of contraception. Condoms can be bought freely at a pharmacy (*gyógyszertár*) or supermarket. Contraceptive and morning-after pills are available by prescription. The number of induced abortions has fallen from 90,000 in 1990 (72 per 100 live births) to 35,000 in 2013, or 40 per 100 live births.

Prostitutes soliciting outdoors are harassed by the police, and brothels as such are illegal. Most of the sex trade is therefore underground, which puts foreign customers especially at some risk of theft or overcharging. But the trade thrives. The Internet now serves as a primary marketing tool, although "classical" methods, such as hotel porters, taxi drivers, coy flyposting, and soliciting in bars, persist.

Children these days don't appear naked in public after they start school at the age of six, but most parents are relaxed about nudity until signs of puberty appear. Most Hungarians find adult nudity distasteful, although there are several nudist bathing places, including Délegyháza, on the borders of Budapest, and some hotels, such as the Gellért, have a naturist sun terrace. There are two naturist camps on Lake Balaton and others dotted around the country.

Awareness of the risks of pedophilia and other sexual abuse has increased substantially in the last twenty years. Traveling on public transportation and walking home, often before the parents are back from work, Hungarian children may appear to be at greater risk than their English-speaking peers, who are so often ferried around in cars. But the statistics match those of Western Europe: risks of violence and abuse are much higher within the family than outside it.

Hungarians are likely to intervene if they see children in trouble, misbehaving, or being ill-treated. On the whole, children by themselves, or in pairs at least, appear to behave better in public than some of their counterparts in Western Europe, and teenage violence, especially against adults, is unusual. But adult protectiveness ceases rather suddenly at puberty. Irate adult passengers quarrel with teenagers on the bus for scarcely perceptible misdemeanors.

MARRIAGE

Marriage in Hungary is often postponed or avoided altogether. As in most of the developing world, the average age for marriage has been rising, and is now around thirty-two for men and twenty-nine for women. Some 55 percent of marriages end in divorce. (This compares with 50 percent in the USA and 42 percent for the UK.)

There is no stigma attached to being born out of wedlock, and little of the social disapproval of cohabitation found in some sections of UK and US society. According to the 2011 census, 910,000 people were cohabiting, unmarried (compared to a married population of 4.5 million). In 2013, almost 46 per cent of births were to unmarried mothers.

The number of children born every year has fallen by 27 percent since 1990. Hungary's population has declined from a peak of 10.7 million in the early 1980s to lower than 9.8 million today.

The number of children falls as the standard of living rises in most developed societies, but this happened earlier and to a greater than average extent in Hungary. There is public awareness of the "demographic problem," but the practical challenge of coping with the future burden of looking after the aged is being sidestepped. The Orbán government, having destroyed the mandatory private pension system in 2011, is seeking to make care for the elderly a legal family obligation.

Almost everyone supports the idea of families having two or three children, but fewer, when it comes down to it, actually do so themselves, mainly because they feel their home would be cramped and they are afraid of the financial sacrifices involved (this, despite generous support in the way of tax allowances for children introduced by the Orbán government). Large families are almost entirely confined to the urban rich and the rural "underclass."

For the population to reproduce itself, every 100 women would need to give birth to 210 children. The present birthrate translates into a mere 147 children (down from 165 in 1990). The shortfall is partly offset by the fact that people are living longer. Life expectancy at birth has risen to seventy-six on average (seventy-two for men and seventy-nine for women), four years less than the OECD on average, and one of the lowest among the OECD countries.

So Hungarians are living longer, but marrying less readily and having fewer children, hence the population is aging. According to one tongue-in-cheek projection, the last Hungarian will die of old age in about four thousand years' time.

chapter six

TIME OUT

BACK TO THE LAND

They call it a *dacha* in Russia and a *gîte* in France. Hungarians call it a *nyaraló*—or sometimes *vikkendház*. It may simply be a patch of garden with a toolshed, but there is often a cottage where its owners can sleep. In fact, some of these "cottages" are positively luxurious—proper houses with swimming pools, wine cellars, vineyards, orchards, and superb views.

Many Hungarians are first- or second-generation city dwellers. A *nyaraló* allows them to get back to their roots, to cultivate a little land, sit in the sun, make strawberry jam or pick apples, go swimming or fishing, or simply chat over the fence to neighbors. The owners are usually part of an extended family, in which the older members do much of the gardening and maintenance, and perhaps move to the *nyaraló* for the whole summer, often joined by children and grandchildren.

The most popular locations are around Balaton, Lake Velence, or the Danube Bend, but *nyaraló* settlements can be seen on hillsides all over the country. That is where millions of Hungarian city dwellers most like to be, and where they do their summer entertaining. Hungarians are a gregarious bunch who enjoy spending time together, often as groups of families.

At the same time, rising disposable incomes have meant an increasing number of Hungarians regularly vacation abroad. The numbers going to the Croatian coast, for example, means a contingent of Hungarian police is regularly stationed in key Dalmatian resorts in the summer to assist in law keeping.

FOOD AND DRINK
Country Cooking
This is about what Hungarians actually eat, especially in the countryside and at the weekend, when there is time to cook—the sort of food that can be found on the menu of an unpretentious, traditional restaurant.

Hungarian families are said to spend, on average, around a third of their disposable income on food and drink. One puzzling statistic shows that older people spend more than younger, but the explanation may be that Hungarians often visit the old folks at home for traditional meals on weekends. If you're ever invited to join them, don't miss the opportunity.

When possible, Hungarians like to eat their main meal in the middle of the day and have cold food in the evening. A typical Hungarian lunch consists of soup and a main course. The sweet course is often left out, but several popular main courses and even some soups are sweet.

The meats of choice are fresh or smoked pork, and chicken. Beef is regularly eaten boiled or stewed, but less

often grilled, as top-quality beef is expensive. Goose, duck, and lamb are occasionally eaten. So are venison, wild boar, and other game. Hungarians are not great fish eaters. Apart from frozen sea fish, the popular choices are carp, salmon, trout, and *fogas* (pike-perch), a Lake Balaton delicacy—but many Hungarians prefer to let a restaurant cope with them.

Fishermen's soup (*halászlé*) is an exception. It's

a spicy brew, dark red with paprika, and should include two or more types of fish, including roe. It's often cooked outside in a cauldron, and is also eaten by many families at Christmas. The classic soup otherwise is a consommé of chicken, beef, or pork (*húsleves*), with vermicelli and plenty of vegetables—carrot, parsley root, celeriac, and onion are the staples. Soup, noodles, and vegetables are placed on the table separately, and diners compile their own bowlful.

On the whole, the Hungarian idea of a square meal is something that's been cooked for a long time in a

good, thick, spicy sauce, with plenty of potato, rice, gnocchi, dumplings, or pasta, and something pickled. Outsize gherkins are popular, pickled in the conventional way in winter, but in summer, often just left out in the sun in a jar with some fennel and a piece of bread in the liquor, to make "leavened" cucumbers (*kovászos uborka*).

Salads take over from pickles in summer and early fall. These are normally served individually—tomato or bell pepper or lettuce or cucumber—as a side dish in a mild liquor of vinegar, water, sugar, and salt. Cucumbers are sometimes given a thicker, pink dressing by adding spice paprika, pepper, and sour cream. The yellow bell peppers can be stronger than they look. Another specialty is a large, flat, sweet, dark-red bell pepper, *paradicsom-paprika* (tomato pepper), with especially thick flesh. The round or pointed chili-like peppers are used in cooking, or ground fresh and added to goulash or fishermen's soup. They can be bought on a string like garlic and hung up in the kitchen.

Garlic, paprika, and marjoram are the commonest flavorings used. The stock cubes of Western Europe are joined in Hungary by goulash cubes and fishermen's-soup cubes.

Sausages of all kinds are eaten cooked or cured. The most famous abroad are Hungarian salami and hard sausages such as *csabai* and *gyulai*. Hungarians themselves probably eat more boiled sausage than any other. *Debreceni*, a thick, fairly spicy, garlicky sausage, is often sold hot at the butcher's, with mild mustard and fresh bread.

Killing a pig is an all-day family occasion, in which the squeamish should not become involved.

The fruits of the labor are a bewildering variety of pork products that can be hung up in the cellar to last a country family through the winter.

Bread, Cheese, and Bacon

Bread is a big and rewarding subject in Hungary. It's eaten at breakfast, lunch, and supper. Hungarians

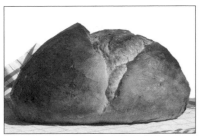

don't share the view that brown bread is morally and nutritionally superior to white. Bread should be white and firm, they say, and in Hungary they're probably right. While brown bread is increasingly popular, the white bread is out of this world.

A popular variation is *félbarna*, which means half-brown, but is actually white bread made with wheat flour. Other popular white breads have maize or potato flour mixed into them. Lots of rolls are eaten: a *zsemle* is fairly soft and round with crumbly crust, while a *kifli* is crescent-shaped and saltier.

Many people take the trouble to go to a traditional baker for their bread. American-style sliced bread is available in supermarkets, and even that seems to be a little better than the original.

Unlike most food in Hungary, much of the cheese is bland and uninteresting. The most popular cheese is Trappist (*trappista*), a dull, rubbery substance. But deep-fried in a breadcrumb batter it turns magically into something delicious, served with tartar sauce.

Liptauer (*körözött*) is a spiced-up, homemade spread of curds made of ewe's milk, with paprika and chopped onion. Curds (*túró*) are the basis for many delightful Hungarian dishes, sweet and savory, including a little refrigerated chocolate bar called a *túró rudi*. Mr. Hershey, are you listening?

Smoked *karaván* cheese is pleasant, and so is the local Emmenthaler, known as Pannónia. Hungarian Cheddar, made in Pécs, is good only for cheeseburgers. Parenyica, however, is a pleasant, half-hard cheese, spun into a spiral and then slightly smoked. Pálpusztai has one of the most revolting smells of any cheese—you have been warned!

Bacon is another field where Anglo-Saxon and Hungarian tastes differ. Hungarians think the fat is the important part of bacon, and often eat it raw, but heavily smoked, seeing the lean of the bacon as a necessary evil, liable to get stuck between your teeth. Take a short, sharp knife, a raw onion, a good piece of Hungarian fat bacon (*szalonna*), a large wine and soda (*nagyfröccs*), and if you're feeling extravagant, a big beef tomato. Nothing could be better for a summer evening meal—but don't tell your cardiologist.

Sour cream is a typical ingredient of many Hungarian dishes—it's used more often than fresh cream, in fact. The heavy, rich, brown bean and boiled-bacon soup known as *Jókai bableves* (a meal in itself) comes with a generous spoonful floating on top. Sour cream is also an ingredient of mushroom *paprikás*, a standby for vegetarians. But its enchantment is greatest in *tökfőzelék*. Made of shredded summer squash (vegetable marrow), this normally dull gourd is transformed into a delicacy by a thick, sour-cream sauce flavored with spice paprika, onion, and chopped dill.

Sweetmeats

Hungarians are fond of crêpes (*palacsinta*). The usual flavors are *túró*, cocoa, or jam. Restaurants like you to order a more elaborate concoction of walnut cream, raisins, rum, and chocolate sauce named after the early twentieth-century restaurateur Károly Gundel. At home, crêpes are often served in a pile, with everyone filling and rolling up their own.

Most hot, sweet dishes are treated as a main course in themselves. They may be quite simple: pasta with ground walnut or poppy seed, and icing sugar, for instance. *Fánk*, often served with apricot jam, are not dissimilar to doughnuts. *Vargabéles* is one of a number of substantial sweet dishes, in this case involving eggs, *túró*, a special pasta, sugar, and raisins. In strudel (*rétes*) the commonest fillings are sweetened cottage cheese, sour cherry, and apple. Pastries from a baker make excellent snacks with coffee.

The creations that have visitors' eyes popping out of their heads are the gâteaux and tortes. You won't find many in self-service stores, however. Hungarians like the ones made by a qualified confectioner (*cukrász*) in a specialist shop, and seldom attempt to make them at home. There are countless outlets up and down the country, especially busy on weekend afternoons. At the pinnacle of the confectioner's profession, and of period

interior design, are the cafés-confiseries of Budapest: the Gerbeaud, the Hauer, the New York, the Művész (handy for the Opera), the Angelika, the Daubner, the Ruszwurm, and the Four Seasons Gresham.

HUNGARIAN WINE

There's probably no other aspect of life where the gulf between the average Magyar and average foreigner is greater than wine—Hungarian wine, that is. For the visitor, it's often a question of "Oh, do you make wine here?" While, for the Hungarian it's a case of "Well, the French make wine too, of course, but I know which I like best."

Under Communism, as with many other industries, winemaking regressed into a drive for quantity over quality. But again, even by the 1980s Hungarian wine makers were striving to reverse this trend, and by the mid-90s hard-working "reform" vintners such as Istvan Szepsey and Attila Gere were winning accolades from foreign wine writers, achieving premium prices for their vintages at home, and inspiring a new generation of high-quality vintners in their wake.

Hungary has twenty-two wine regions or sub-regions, but without doubt it is the Tokaj region, some 150 miles to the northeast of Budapest, and its honey-sweet dessert *aszú* wines for which Hungary is most famous—and which will likely form the basis for the after-dinner toast for any visiting foreign business delegation. It is Tokaj, too, that has attracted the most interest from foreign investors, with French, Spanish, British and even Japanese taking stakes in its wineries in the early 1990s.

Numerous wine festivals are held throughout the country in the summer and fall, the grandest being Budapest's in early September. However, anyone wanting to taste in a more relaxed and affordable environment would do well to seek out a provincial event. More sedate still, many wine shops in the capital offer tastings and talks; or, since every region has been investing in tourism facilities in the past decade, a weekend trip to explore and meet vintners on their home turf can be a very enjoyable experience.

EATING OUT

Restaurant and café culture has exploded in Hungary during the past ten to fifteen years, supported by a growing middle class at home, expatriate Magyars returning home with money earned abroad, and a booming tourism sector based on low-cost airlines.

Naturally, while the provinces have played a part in the transformation, it is Budapest that has been the trendsetter, with whole sectors of the capital buzzing with diners and party-goers every summer evening—and many a winter one too.

The epicenter of this revolution is in the streets and alleyways of Budapest VI and VII districts behind the Great Synagogue, where many so-called "ruin pubs" began life. These establishments typically began as temporary affairs in buildings awaiting renovation (or demolition), and shunned any pretensions of thoughtful décor or designer furniture: guests would seat themselves on worn-out sofas, surrounded by unplastered brick walls—but at least the bar staff would smile (and usually speak English). The affordable, no-frills service, created for students and a motley Bohemian clientele, quickly attracted tourists, and in turn more traditional eateries fell over one another to join the fun, and share the profits.

Simultaneously, and at the more refined end of the hospitality sector, the better hotels were working hard to improve their dining experience, while not a few nouveau-riche business folk teamed up with more innovative Hungarian chefs (many of whom had worked abroad) to set up a string of fine-dining ventures, mainly in Pest, but also on the Buda side.

Throw in a few wine bars and pubs stocked with craft beers, and the result is a cacophony of diners, bistros, and Bohemian dives offering a broad mix

of styles and fares leaving the hungry visitor with a choice from the bargain-basement pizza pusher to any one of twenty-nine institutions listed in the 2016 *Michelin Guide*, five of which boast a one-star rating.

TRIED AND TESTED
As an indication of the choice and quality on hand, of a group of eight adequately wealthy Magyar and foreign diners canvassed by *Culture Smart!* as to their favorite eateries, none chose any of the Michelin-starred outlets. Among those recommended of the hundreds available:

- Pomodoro (Italian): Real Italian, a wide selection of really fresh fish from Italy, and excellent ambience.
- Rosenstein (Hungarian–Jewish): Huge selection of different meals (poultry, fish, veal, beef), excellent goose liver and Hungarian fish soup. Next to a police station with a jail, in a neighborhood where you do not expect a good restaurant.
- Bock Bisztro (Hungarian): Most sophisticated Hungarian cuisine; highly calorific.
- Olympia (Hungarian): More affordable than the above, and their cuisine and selection is excellent. Cards not accepted.
- Café Kör: Favorite for business lunches downtown. Duck leg and pan fried chicken leg both excellent.
- Zeller Bistro: Students' favorite.

Recommendations in the print media are not all reliable: much of the information consists of advertisements, for which the restaurants pay. Having said that, there are millions of good lunches waiting to be eaten—restaurant food in Hungary tends to be at its best around 1:00 p.m. After that, it's probably better to choose from the "freshly made" (*frissensültek*) section of the bill of fare rather than the "ready-made" (*készételek*). Rice and pasta, for instance, will have lost much of their moisture content by mid-afternoon.

Most restaurants, with or without pretensions, will cost about half what it would in Western Europe, but as everywhere, the tourist districts have their over-priced tourist venues, and that includes the Buda Castle District in particular.

For really good value, consider having the set meal, confusingly known as the *menü*. This normally consists of soup, a smaller portion of a main course, and some kind of sweet dish, perhaps fruit or a slice of cake. In unpretentious Budapest restaurants, this will normally cost in the range of Ft 1,000–Ft 1,300 (that is, US $4–5, including 10 percent tip), and even less outside the capital.

This also gets over one of the problems in Hungarian restaurants these days. There's tough competition for customers, and one competitive weapon that's used is outsized portions, so that many customers can't cope with more than the main course, whereas Hungarian food is meant to be enjoyed as a succession of dishes, not as one big plateful

Now, let's say you've been recommended a good restaurant. Hungarian etiquette dictates that the host should walk in first and attract the attention of the staff. Even in quite modest establishments, there'll be someone to show you to a table. By all means state a preference and see if you can sit at the table that looks best. Two waiters will come—one for the drinks and one for the food. Waiters' wine recommendations are usually useful and fair. Enjoy your meal, and don't hurry. If it's dinner you're having, stay all evening if you wish, ordering this and that from time to time.

Gypsy bands are out of fashion, but no visit to Hungary is really complete without one. They're fascinating to watch, especially the cimbalom—a vast concert dulcimer whose strings are struck with sticks like a xylophone. Any tune in the world can be converted into Hungarian Gypsy music at the drop of a hat. So as the night draws on, don't be shy about exhibiting your karaoke talents when the leader (*primás*) comes to your table and plays the number of your choice to your lady love. Budapest restaurants famous for hosting gypsy bands include the Kárpátia and Kéhli.

IN YOUR CUPS

Elderly Australians who can remember when the bars in Victoria closed at six might enjoy visiting a Hungarian *kocsma* (pub), *italbolt* (drink shop), or *borozó* (wine bar), with its uniquely dingy, smoky ambience—despite modern non-smoking laws. They're not recommended to anyone else. Beer, wine, and the local spirit, *pálinka*, are drunk by men at great speed, and that's that. No food—other, perhaps, than a cheese *szendvics*. Some villages have nothing else, mind you, so you may need to go into one from time to time. Pay as you drink. Most close about 9:00 p.m.

One step up the ladder is the *presszó*. This may still have some pretensions as a place to have an espresso coffee and eat a cake, but the main business is drink. There is usually table service. They come into their

TIPPING

The amount to tip is easy—10 to15 percent of
the bill. Check the bill first because (a) not a few
establishments "somehow" manage to add an
extra item and (b) many now include a service
charge as standard. More important is how to tip.
Only one waiter can give bills—you'll notice the
wallet in his trouser pocket—but you can ask any
of the staff, "*Fizetni szeretnék*" ("I'd like to pay").

Add your percentage, round up the sum, and
tell the waiter how much you're prepared to
pay, including the tip. Note that—as the official
tourism site warns—you should beware of saying
"thank you" as you hand over your cash; most
waiters/waitresses will take this to mean that
they don't need to give any change at all! This
can lead to an unpleasant misunderstanding
while you wait for change that never comes.

It's always better to pay in local currency.
All except the most local restaurants take cards
today, but always check beforehand that the
system is working: some seem to suffer from
dodgy card-readers all too frequently.

There's no need to tip other staff (there may
be a small fixed charge to use the restroom).
The exception is live music. The violinist
who serenaded your loved one, or the pianist
who obligingly played your favorite number,
doesn't share the handout at the end of the day.
Depending on the quality of venue and serenade
(and while not obligatory) 1,000–3,000 forints is
appropriate, inserted near the bridge of the violin
or tucked behind the piano's open fallboard.

For taxi drivers, see page 135.

own in the summer, when it's pleasant to sit outside. This is a broad category and includes plenty of civilized places to drink or meet your friends, unless the television's on too loud. They stay open till 11:00 p.m. or later. Pay the waitstaff when you leave, unless you're just having a quickie at the counter.

A brasserie (*söröző*) sells beer and other drinks and the kind of grilled food that's good after a hard day's work. Cubicles in knotty pinewood would be typical. One of these is probably the best place to walk into with the family in a strange town. Kitchens close about 9:00 p.m., but the drinking goes on later.

Drinking in Public
There is a law against drinking alcohol in the street and in various other public places in Hungary, although it is only enforced at the discretion of local authorities.

Café Life
Café life in the Austro-Hungarian sense has been undergoing a renaissance in Budapest and some other cities. The word to look for over the door is *kávé*,

or *kávéház*. Expect large numbers of young people lingering over coffee and drinks and talking at the tops of their voices. Most cafés sell a limited range of food, competently cooked and served. Many stay open until the small hours.

Of course, there are plenty of places that don't really fit into any of these categories. For a pleasant evening with friends, a modest restaurant is probably the most convenient and comfortable. Kitchens tend to close by 10:00 p.m., after which the waiters begin crumb-shaking rituals designed to speed the parting guests.

BOX OFFICE BARGAINS

Budapest is paradise for fans of opera, ballet, and classical music, the ticket prices are very good value, and there are no extras apart from a tip of a couple of hundred forints at the cloakroom as you pick up your things when you leave.

Take the Opera (Magyar Állami Operaház)—one of the world's great late-nineteenth-century theater buildings. The original-language repertoire includes

good doses of Mozart, Verdi, Puccini, and Wagner, well sung by Hungarian and foreign guest stars, sprinkled with lesser-known Hungarian greats (Erkel, Bartók, Ránki), well-chosen twentieth-century works (Janacek, Prokofiev, Shostakovich, Britten), and classical and modern ballets, along with the occasional modern musical. Some productions are at the recently renovated Erkel Theater, however, built in 1910–11.

Many of the operettas at the Budapest Operetta Theater, and some others, offer English-language surtitles above the stage. Check to be sure.

The most expensive opera ticket is about Ft 25,000 (US $90) and the cheapest (certain seats for some matinees) Ft 500 (US $1.80). Hungarians usually buy subscriptions for several performances, which offer price reductions and a chance to book the same seats year after year.

Visually, the best place in Budapest to listen to a symphony or choral music is the main hall of the

Academy of Music (Zeneakadémia). The ambience, the gilt, the organ pipes, the proportions—all divine, and now looking stunning after a total renovation.

The Budapest Convention Center (1980s) has dull acoustics. The National Concert Hall by the Danube, universally known as MUPA, usually has excellent programs. However, its location, in south Pest, is a little bit off the beaten path, and taxi pickups need careful arranging.

There are four main symphony orchestras in Budapest, and other full-time orchestras in the main provincial cities. There are strong traditions of chamber music as well, so that hardly a night passes without a concert or a recital somewhere. Other good performances of interest are given at the Operetta (operettas and musicals, but in Hungarian) and the Budai Vigadó (exuberant folk-dance shows).

Talking of exhuberant performances, don't miss the Budapest Gypsy Symphony Orchestra (aka the 100-member Gypsy Orchestra—100 Tagú Cigányzenekar) if it's playing anywhere near you.

FOLK, ROCK, AND JAZZ

Much to the chagrin of the Communist authorities, Hungarian youth took to Western jazz–rock–pop cultures in a big way from the 1950s on. Three bands in particular, Metro, Illés, and Omega, stand out as home-grown icons during the 1960s and early '70s.

The year 1983 saw the first performance of *István, a király*, a rock opera written by Levente Szörényi (music) and János Bródy (lyrics). Loosely based on the tenth-century struggle between the Christianizing King Stephen and Koppány, his pagan rival, the work touched national feelings, becoming an instant success, and is still revered.

Ironically, despite official concerns, Hungary was almost certainly the most open Warsaw Pact state in terms of allowing Western groups to visit. One youth—later to become the Hungarian ambassador to Washington—remembers waiting outside the hotel to meet the English progressive rock band Traffic in 1967—successfully inviting them down to his family holiday home on Balaton. Jethro Tull first visited in the early 1980s and have made Budapest a regular tour venue ever since. Late in the decade, Queen stormed into Budapest, to be followed in the democratic era by stars such as Yes, Bob Dylan, Paul Simon, Rod Stewart, and the Rolling Stones. Nowadays, foreign stars tend to focus on the summer music festivals, such as the Sziget and Volt.

Modern domestic headliners include rock band Kiscsillag, pop act Wellhello, and up-and-coming alternative pop artist Balázs Szabó.

Old-timers such as Pál Utcai Fiúk (classic progressive rock) and DJ Palotai, the doyen of Magyar electronic music, still play the odd concert. Anyone into the blues should look out for Mátyás Prbiojszki (great blues harp) and guitarist Tibor Tátrai.

Jazz —A Surprise Genre on the Danube

Jazz lovers will be surprised to learn that Hungary has a vibrant jazz scene. All the jazz styles from Dixieland to avant-garde can be heard in Budapest. The best clubs to go to are the Budapest Jazz Club and the Opus Club. Entry fees are moderate by Western standards, as are the associated food and drinks.

HUNGARIAN "DANCE HOUSE," AN EXEMPLARY MUSIC REVIVAL MOVEMENT

Filtering down from the court musicians of the Renaissance to the peasantry, each region of Transylvania, today in Romania, has its own variant of beautiful and noble dance music played on fiddle, viola, and bass.

In the late 1960s and early '70s, Hungarian musicians Ferenc Sebő and Béla Halmos heard some on the radio—this at a time under Communism when Hungarian music was forbidden in Romania and frowned upon in Hungary as nationalistic. It was completely unknown to them.

Sebő and Halmos visited Transylvania and—at some risk to themselves and the local musicians—learned to play the music from both Roma and ethnic Magyar musicians. They returned to Hungary, and began playing at local halls, where dance evenings became very popular.

While the government turned a blind eye and cupped a deaf ear, countless young people and intellectuals attended and learned the dances, among them then teenager Márta Sebestyén and other members of what became the band Muzsikás, who went on to popularize the genre globally.

These days the dance house movement continues to flourish, with live music at a variety of dance houses nearly every night of the week. In summer, there are dance house camps.

You can easily join in as there is always a dance teacher in attendance. The best are at

Arany János utca 10 on a Saturday evening (District V) and the Fono Music House on Sztregova utca, District XI, on Wednesdays. See www.tanchaz.hu for others.

The movement has received a cultural heritage award from UNESCO for its dance teaching methods.

GALLERIES AND MUSEUMS

There are three places in Budapest that art lovers mustn't miss. Normally speaking, the first is the Museum of Fine Arts (Szépművészeti Múzeum), which has a fine collection of European paintings. However, at the time of writing, this museum is under renovation, scheduled to reopen in 2018. Until then, the collection is on show at the Hungarian National Gallery, except for any paintings in storage or exhibited on tour.

Three of the most famous exhibits are Raphael's *Esterházy Madonna*, Goya's *Girl Carrying Water*, and Delacroix's exquisite *Horse Frightened by Lightning*. Monet, Manet, Cézanne, Renoir, Gauguin, Chagall, Rembrandt, and many others are represented.

Turning to the second, the Hungarian National

Gallery in Buda Castle boasts the works of Hungarian artists down the ages, some of which are astonishingly good and rarely exhibited outside the country. Of earlier masters, look especially for Miklós Barabás (1810–98), József Borsos (1821–83), Viktor Madarász (1830–1917), Mihály Munkácsy (1844–1900), and Tivadar Csontváry Kosztka (1853–1919), as well as avant-garde "activists" of the 1920s such as Béla Uitz (1887–1972) and Lajos Kassák (1887–1967).

The third place is the Opera building, completed in 1884. The frescoes that clothe most of the public areas are remarkable compositions by three masters of Hungarian historicism, Károly Lotz, Bertalan Székely, and Mór Than.

On the whole, museums and galleries in Hungary tend to be small and specialized, but there are some particularly interesting collections.

Memento Park (commonly known as the Communist statue park) is an open-air sculpture museum displaying the Socialist Realist work of the Communist period, while also offering a host of accompanying "retro-red" activities. Located at Diósd, eight miles south of Budapest, it is a bit of a hike by public transport, but many find it worth the effort.

Would-be engine drivers can fulfill their dream at the Railway Museum Park, in north Budapest. Believed to the largest of its kind in Europe, with over fifty locomotives on show, the former locomotive depot hosts regular special events, including an international railway jamboree each September.

Across the river, Budapest's District III has some gems, among them the Goldberger Textile

Collection, a prizewinning museum on the site of the prewar Goldberger textile factory. It is beautifully laid out and displays the production processes from the traditional hand-printed blue and white calico to the elegant silks worn by fashionable women in the 1930s. Plenty of colorful swatches, a feast for the eyes.

Up the road is the Victor Vasarely Collection, which draws steady numbers. For anyone seeking out some culture and history behind alcoholic drinks, both the Zwack Unicum Heritage Center (District IX) and the Dreher Brewery and Museum, in Kobanya (District X) offer intriguing visits.

Outside Budapest, notable attractions include the Museum of Modern Art in Pécs, the Museum of Naive Artists in Kecskemét, the Catholic collections in Esztergom, and the Serbian one in Szentendre.

SPORTS AND PASTIMES

Most Hungarians enjoy watching sports on television, but relatively few take part after the age of twenty-five. By far the most popular spectator sport is soccer (*foci*). The legendary Golden Team (Aranycsapat) walked off with the 1952 Olympic trophy and famously trounced England 6–3 at Wembley—the first time England had lost at home to a side from outside the UK—in 1953, before beating them 7–1 at home the next year and reaching the World Cup finals. To put it another way, the Golden Team scored 220 goals in fifty-one matches between June 1950 and November 1955.

But "how are the mighty fallen." True, the national team reached the finals of the UEFA European Football Championship finals in 2016, winning through to the last sixteen, including a thrilling 3–3 draw against Portugal, the eventual winners. But while this run thrilled Magyars around the globe, it represented the only appreciable international success since 1986, when Hungary managed to qualify for the World Championships in Mexico.

It also brought joy for Viktor Orbán—the prime minister who wanted to be a professional footballer until his father insisted he go to university. Since 2010, his tax policies have meant that corporations receive tax-breaks when directing millions of euros in donations to sports clubs in general, and soccer clubs in particular.

Despite the enthusiasm and money, most Hungarian club soccer matches today attract pitiful crowds of a couple of hundred. The principal exception to this trend is Ferencváros, the main "protest" team under Communism, who play in

the spanking-swanky Groupama Aréna stadium in Budapest District IX—though it too is rarely more than one-third full for ordinary league matches, which take place most weekends during the season, that is July to December and February to May.

However, there are several sports in which Hungary often does well in world championships and at the Olympics, notably canoeing, handball, water polo, swimming, pentathlon, fencing, and shooting.

The focus of sporting activity in Hungary are the sports clubs all over the country, which may cover both amateur and professional players. Many clubs are centered on Hungarian League soccer teams. These clubs have plenty of facilities for sports at an amateur level. So do local clubs, often attached to a school gym, and you don't need to be connected with the school to take part. All these facilities are cheap by European or North American standards.

A decade ago, golf was touted as the game of the future, with any number of courses supposedly in the planning stages. In the event, the sport has struggled to attract domestic players. There are ten eighteen-hole golf courses with open membership, mostly around Budapest and in the environs of Lake Balaton, along with a handful of nine-hole courses. Arguably the green fees, which tend to be set at international levels, form one barrier to domestic membership.

Riding and tennis are readily available, popular, and quite reasonably priced. One place of pilgrimage for horse riders is Szilvásvárad, a small town 19 miles (30 km) north of Eger, famous for its stud of Lipizzaner horses.

There is good windsurfing, kitesurfing, and sailing on Lake Balaton, and waterskiing on Lake Tisza.

 Attractive places for canoeing include the Szigetköz stretch of the Danube and around the wine region of Tokaj, on the Tisza River.

From October to February you can skate on the lake in the Városliget, a park in the middle of

Budapest. There are smaller rinks at several shopping centers. Ten-pin bowling is popular, and is also played competitively.

Chess is very popular, boosted by the phenomenal global success of the three Polgár sisters in the period 1985–2015. Although none play competitively today, Judit, the youngest, and easily the most successful female player of all time, remains very active in promoting the sport in Hungary and internationally.

There are 322 chess clubs affiliated with the Hungarian Chess Federation (Magyar Sakkszövetség), and there are plenty of people to play a game of chess with you in the summer in Budapest parks.

SAVING AND SPENDING

Shops, banks, post offices, and utility customer services have improved beyond all recognition since the Communist era, and any town worthy of the name will boast at least one Western-brand supermarket, usually Tesco, Spar, or Auchan, plus competition from home-grown competitors, such as CBA.

Budapest, in particular, saw an explosion of shopping malls and hypermarkets in 1995–2005. Malls certainly have convenience and variety on their side, but the shops in them tend to be more expensive than the solo hypermarkets on the edge of towns.

Yet, for all the external trappings, the new facilities still leave something to be desired, often in terms of service with a smile, and sometimes with respect to quality of produce. Even in swish Budapest malls it may prove difficult to find sales staff with more than a smattering of English.

Banks are pretty much on a par with their Western counterparts, with ATMs commonplace, but accounts and services typically come with a litany of charges—even for checking one's account at an ATM. Nor does it help that the state imposes a tax on almost all transactions. (This is not levied directly on accounts, but inevitably finds its way to the customer.)

SHOPPING FOR PLEASURE

The most enjoyable places to shop are the market halls of Budapest and some other cities. The units vary from full-scale shops to one little peasant woman selling a handful of vegetables or a few jars of honey. At the Central Market Hall (Nagycsarnok) of Pest—a tourist

favorite—there are ten or twelve rival traders selling live freshwater fish, and even an Asian deli in the basement. There are also regular special events, such as national food days that feature food from Japan to Mexico, and much in between. The snack stands on the iron galleries above are among the best fast-food bargains in the city. Go native and order wine and soda (*fröccs*) to wash them down.

The market in District V (at the back of the US embassy) is less visited, but has equally varied food stalls in the gallery offering delicious, affordable fare.

Also enjoyable are the craft markets held from time to time in the Buda Castle District and elsewhere, especially in the summer, often in combination with wine festivals. There's a big Christmas one in Vörösmarty tér, in the center of Pest.

INTO THE COUNTRYSIDE

There are marked trails for hikers in many country areas, especially woodland. These marks, painted on trees and walls, are shown on special hiking maps, but often by the initial of the color in Hungarian (K=blue, S=yellow, P=red, Z=green). The longest and most celebrated trail is the Blue Tour (Kék túra), which stretches right across the country. Among the handiest and most popular areas for a walk on the wild side are the Buda Hills, overlooking Budapest.

Budapest has become a significant urban cycling city, now boasting some 125 miles (200 km) of cycle paths, and sits astride EuroVelo route 6. Cyclists need their wits about them, however, as cycle paths are often obstructed by wayward pedestrians and parked cars. At the same time, cyclists could show better respect for the law and their fellow man— they frequently ride illegally at dangerous speeds on pedestrian sidewalks.

The rest of the country is crisscrossed by designated cycle paths or recommended country lanes, shown on several national road atlases. One good trip is an Austro-Hungarian ride around Lake Fertő— reasonably flat, very scenic, and a total of about 80–90 miles (130–40 km), with plenty of beaches and facilities by the wayside. Renting a bike usually costs about 2,500 forints (US $9) a day.

Hungary is famed for its love of horses and its equestrian skills, and there are many riding stables offering horses for experienced riders and lessons for novices. Many of these offer up to week-long packages, with prices generally cheaper than in Western Europe, especially if booked locally.

Hungary is also an ideal place for bird-watching. It has a wide range of habitats and lies at a crossroads of busy migration routes. Some 365 species have been officially recorded. The best guide is Gerard Gorman's *Birds of Hungary*.

There are well-stocked lakes, rivers, and reservoirs for freshwater fishing, and catches are famous for their variety and flavor, especially for carp and catfish. Fishing seasons vary for species and locations. Licenses are bought locally and reasonably priced. Angling is very popular.

Hunting (which means shooting, not chasing by huntsmen and hounds, which is not practiced) has deep roots in Hungary—and the sport attracts visitors from far and wide, including Arabia. The game includes roe, red and fallow deer, wild boar, moufflon (wild sheep), and various birds and waterfowl. Permanent residents may take the hunting exam, buy third-party insurance, and join the Hungarian National Hunting Chamber. Visitors must present a home hunting license to the Chamber. Unfortunately, it is not legal at present to rent guns; prospective hunters must have their own.

Rock climbers, at all levels, will find interesting cliff faces and artificial climbing walls.

OFF THE BEATEN PATH
Rural Hungary is sparsely populated and uniquely attractive. Visitors find the traditional peasant cottage particularly enticing. Each district has its own variant, but in most parts it consists of two or three rooms and a kitchen arranged side by side, at right angles to the road, on a relatively long, narrow plot of land. Farm buildings, orchard, and a narrow strip of farmland continue beyond. An open fire with a smoke hole in the roof above the kitchen gave way

to a stove and a proper chimney in the early twentieth century. Walls are often made of mud bricks on a masonry foundation, and roofs may be of thatch, tiles, or occasionally shingles.

There is a complete village of such cottages at Hollókő in Nógrád County, all built in traditional style after a fire in 1909, in the folk style of the district. They are grouped around a tiny church in the shadow of a ruined medieval castle. Several of them are available to rent. Typical cottages and country buildings have been transported from various parts of the country and rebuilt as a national open-air museum (*skanzen*) outside Szentendre, twenty miles north of Budapest. There are similar local collections in Szombathely and elsewhere, but almost all Hungarian villages still have some traditional cottages.

Doing up a country cottage is popular among wealthier Hungarians and foreign buyers. There are long traditions of Hungarians owning a small garden or a second home if they can afford it.

BALATON

Lake Balaton has an area of 232 square miles (600 sq. km), a length of 48 miles (77 km), a breadth of 1–9 miles (1.5–14 km), a depth of less than 13 feet (4 m) in most places and nowhere more than 38 feet (11.5 m), and a shoreline of around 125 miles (200 km)—but saying all this is to miss the point. Balaton ("Balcsi" to its friends) is more than a lake, it's a state of mind. Although more people go to the Adriatic coast than to Balaton nowadays, it's still synonymous to Hungarians with a traditional summer vacation on the beach.

The season is only eight to ten weeks long, prices are fairly high (for Hungary), the beaches are sometimes crowded, and many of the forty or so resorts are nondescript in appearance, but choose carefully (Balatonfüred, Balatonföldvár, Tihany, or the hilly shore onward to Keszthely), and Balaton will work its magic. The nearest resorts are less than sixty miles (96 km) from Budapest.

The water is silky, a slightly milky gray, and as clean as the Adriatic. It heats up to 77°–80°F (25°–27°C) or more on a summer's day. And in winter—another good time for a visit—it freezes quickly for skating or gadding about on the local type of hand-pulled sleigh—a *fakutya* or "wooden dog," really a kitchen chair on runners propelled with short ski sticks.

Vacationing at Balaton began in a modest way in the early nineteenth century, around such places as Balatonfüred, which has medicinal springs said to be good for heart disease. The Helikon arts festival at Keszthely took place for the first time in 1817. Bathing in the lake itself became popular with the wealthy in the 1830s. Balaton vacations became affordable for all in the Communist period, if not available to all at the trade union hostels that mushroomed in the 1960s. Vouchers were distributed to "workers," largely according to an elaborate system of sociopolitical points. Many of these hostels still survive, offering simple accommodation with full board at reasonable cost, usually to members of a company, institution, association, or school.

TIME FOR A SWIM
There are lots of wonderful places to bathe in Hungary. Three of the best are a bathing and swimming complex, a natural thermal lake, and a beach beneath an extinct volcano.

Budapest's Császár-Komjádi complex, known locally as the Csaszi, dates from Turkish times. It contains the best pools for serious swimmers. There are five pools, three in the open air. The Császár has the Turkish baths, while the Lukács is a delightful nineteenth-century establishment. The Szechenyi Baths, located in the City Park, are probably the most popular bathing facilities in Budapest. Locals and tourists alike swim, soak, and sauna in this multipooled, neo-Baroque facility in all weathers.

The Healing Lake (Gyógy-tó) at Hévíz, near Lake Balaton, is 130 feet (39.5 m) deep and the second-largest thermal lake in the world. The slightly radioactive water changes every two days, but remains at least 80°F (27°C) at the surface. This is a chance to swim among red tropical water lilies below Victorian bathhouses.

The third tip is to relax in the silky water of Balaton off the beach at Szigliget and gaze up at the extinct volcano of Badacsony, where the best wines of the region grow. Then you can sample the wines and fried Balaton fish—try the *fogas* (pike-perch)—at any of a dozen restaurants.

chapter **seven**

TRAVEL, HEALTH, & SAFETY

AIRPORTS

The vast majority of commercial flights operate from Budapest's Liszt Ferenc International Airport, still called by its former name of Ferihegy by many. All flights are now handled by Terminals 2A and 2B, four minutes walk from each other, and 15 miles (24 km) from the city.

The airport is served by regulated taxis, with a fare to the city typically close to Ft 8,000 (US $29). A bus service runs to central Budapest every thirty minutes for Ft 900 (US $3.50). The minibus service is no longer so reasonable: budget-minded travelers use the bus and metro to get to the city center for a bargain Ft 700 (US $2.50). Note that the money changing booths at the airport offer appallingly bad rates.

A few international flights use Debrecen airport. The airport at Sármellék, at the southern end of Balaton, known today as Hévíz–Balaton Airport, has limited seasonal flights. There are no scheduled internal passenger flights in Hungary.

PUBLIC TRANSPORTATION

Hungary has an extensive system of public transportation, though of variable standard. One Intercity train may be modern, smooth-riding, air-conditioned stock, and an hour later a following service may be grubby, shunting from side to side, with windows wide open to provide some relief from the summer heat. Buses are sometimes too fast for comfort.

Hungarian State Railways (MÁV) boasts a mainly radial network of just below 5,000 route-miles (8,000 km), centered on Budapest. International trains to Vienna and beyond, branded Railjet, offer the swishest flagship services. Intercity services to major cities are cleaner, frequent, fairly fast, and reliable. An express supplement and seat ticket are usually payable on fast services. Hungarian and EU citizens over sixty-five are entitled to free domestic travel but must purchase seat tickets, if applicable.

Long-distance bus services are run by the Volán group of companies. On intercity routes, trains tend to be more frequent, a little faster and marginally more expensive than buses—though either way, fares are very affordable by international standards.

Tickets are bought before boarding, from a ticket office, by phone, or on the Internet. Some stations have ticket machines, with instructions in English.

Budapest's Western (Nyugati) and Eastern (Keleti) railway termini are remarkable pieces of nineteenth-century architecture. The former was designed by the Eiffel company and completed in 1877. The old station restaurant with its ornate cast ironwork is probably the most elegant branch of McDonald's in Europe. The Southern station (Déli) is spacious, functional, Communist-era concrete—but the international ticket office there is underused, and a good place for buying tickets—even if most such trains arrive and depart from Keleti.

Water transportation is more limited. There are passenger services upstream from Budapest on the

Danube and on Lake Balaton between spring and fall, and a hydrofoil up the Danube to Vienna.

PUNCH AND RIDE

Budapest's public transportation system is as eclectic as the city's architecture: buses, streetcars (trams), trolleybuses, suburban trains, underground railways, a funicular, a rack railway, a chairlift (up the Buda Hills), and a narrow-gauge children's railway. Bicycle hire, in the form of the so-called Mol "Bubi" system, is cheap and tourist friendly.

For local public transportation, passengers need to

buy individual tickets, a book of tickets, or a pass before boarding—although on some bus lines, drivers now sell tickets at a premium price. Tickets must be validated on boarding the vehicle. In Budapest, this means pushing the ticket—with its grid of numbers in front and facing up—into a slot for punching or canceling. This has to be done at the station barrier on the Budapest Metro. Gruff, plain-clothes inspectors levy spot fines on those they catch without a valid ticket. They typically comprehend, but steadfastly do not accept: "I don't understand Hungarian."

The funicular runs from Clark Ádám tér at the Buda end of the Chain Bridge up to the Royal Palace of Buda. Originally built to provide workers with cheap access up the hill, today it is, frankly, poor value. True, the cars are nicely restored, but with return tickets at roughly US $7 for the short ride, no worker would join the line when the same (beautiful) view can be had by catching a bus into the castle and walking down the bank.

The underground railway line M1 was the first on continental Europe when it opened in 1896, and Emperor–King Francis Joseph himself had a ride. M2 and M3 were largely built in the Communist era; M4 opened only in 2014.

An interesting trip for transportation enthusiasts is to take the rack railway (*fogaskerekű*, commonly mistranslated as cog-wheel railway) from Városmajor, two tram stops from Széll Kálmán tér, up Sváb-hegy. This opened in 1874. It proceeds rather slowly and noisily up 4,082 yards (3,733 m) of steep gradient in about fifteen minutes. It's then a short walk to the terminus of the Children's Railway (*gyermekvasút*), for a brief ride through the woods to Hűvösvölgy. Built in 1948, the railway is run (under adult supervision) by child volunteers in immaculate railway uniforms.

TAXIS

All licensed taxis are painted yellow, air-conditioned, and accept bank cards. The tariffs are fixed rate, but no longer as cheap as they once were, with a US $2 base fare plus a US $1 charge per kilometer. Despite the supposedly strict regulatory regime, the tourist authorities still advise not to hail a taxi on the streets. The government banned Uber in 2016 after protests by traditional taxi drivers—an ironic move from an administration that claims to support innovation.

Tipping was a standard 10 percent, but with recent increases in fares, tipping need not be so generous. Visitors can strike deals for half-day or day trips.

ON THE ROAD

Hungary has created an excellent expressway system over the past twenty-five years, with just over 1,000 miles (1,609 km) of motorways. This, similar to the railway network, is centered on Budapest. Drivers have to pay to use almost all the expressways, except for the M0 orbital motorway around the capital. Any driver not buying the electronic vignette in advance will almost certainly be fined. Details of vignette fees may be found online. The regular roads are not always so well maintained, particularly in cities.

The minimum age for a driver's license is seventeen, but some car rental companies insist on a minimum age limit of nineteen or twenty-one, and all insist any license must have been held for more than a year.

European licenses are valid in Hungary, but visitors from most non-European countries, including the USA, Canada, and Australia, must have an International Driver's Permit.

Hungary uses the international system of road signs and markings common throughout Europe.

Remember the so-called "right-hand rule"—drivers must give way to the right at unmarked junctions.

Low-beam, or dipped headlights are compulsory even in daytime outside built-up areas. Full-beam headlights are prohibited in built-up areas at night. A first-aid kit and a warning triangle must be carried in the car. The main speed limits are 31 mph (50 kmph) in built-up areas (within the black-on-white city-limit signs), 56 mph (90 kmph) outside built-up areas, 68 mph (110 kmph) on limited-access trunk roads, and 80 mph (130 kmph) on freeways.

There are pay-and-display parking systems in Budapest and many other towns.

Driving Culture

Although the quality of driving in Hungary has improved in the past decade, for many North Americans and Britons the driving culture in Hungary seems both aggressive and sometimes downright dangerous. A significant minority of local drivers will overtake, regardless of red traffic lights 100 meters ahead. They will step on the gas, overtake—don't expect a signal—and brake it all way in a matter of ten seconds, all to be one space ahead.

This aggressive nature is reflected in the statistics: in 2014, there were 626 road deaths in Hungary, equating to 6.3 road deaths per 100,000 of population. In the UK, with far higher car usage, there were 2.9 road deaths per 100,000 people in the same year.

The police are often used in the most inefficient manner. Instead of targeting dangerous drivers, they may stop a car for no apparent reason, and find ingenious reasons to levy fines. They do this by giving the driver a yellow ticket for a sum to be paid at a post office. There is a system of black marks, so that successive offenses, even minor ones, may lead to confiscation of the driver's license. The permitted blood alcohol limit is zero.

When an accident occurs, the police must be called if there is personal injury or if the drivers involved can't agree on who is to blame. Otherwise the drivers may simply exchange insurance documents or reach a private agreement.

EMERGENCY NUMBERS
Fire/police/ambulance 112
The Automobile Club 188

However, if you are the innocent party, some old hands advise calling the police, however small the damage. There is a paper that the involved parties need to fill in, but they are free to recall their written statement at any time (by saying that they were threatened or confused). With the police present, it prevents the guilty party recalling the statement.

OUT FOR THE DAY

It is worth mentioning a few excursion destinations out of Budapest. Wherever you go, take time to sit and eat in a local restaurant—they're usually good value, even compared with Budapest. The same applies to private accommodation, which is plentiful.

By public transportation, you can visit Szentendre (quaint streets, Serbian churches, Serbian museum, art); Esztergom (basilica, churches, Christian museum, castle ruins, and eighteenth-century town); Vácrátót

A Winter's Day

A couple of days after Christmas we set out to see one of Hungary's buried treasures, and to find a good restaurant. Once out of Budapest, we were almost on our own for a two-hour drive down a winding road, with the Balaton Uplands on our left. Then we reached the dusty, half-deserted little town of Sümeg. Our aim was to go into the parish church there, but it was locked. We wandered about, passing a dilapidated Baroque mansion and the local museum. An elderly lady asked us what we were looking for. We told her. "Oh, there he goes!" she cried, pointing to a tall young man carrying shopping bags—the sexton! Of course he would let us into the church and share with us his enthusiasm for the frescoes. There was just enough wintry light to see them—the finest work of Franz Anton Maulbertsch (1724–95).

We found half the town having a late lunch in a barn of a restaurant at the foot of Sümeg's medieval castle, where we had an excellent meal.

Sümeg Castle, now a museum, saw action in the conflicts with both the Ottoman Turks and the Austrians. It is now considered one of the best-restored fortresses in Hungary.

(vast, unkempt botanical gardens); Gödöllő (restored royal summer palace), and two a little further afield: Kecskemét (Art Nouveau architecture, toy museum, *pálinka* museum, and naive art); and Herend (porcelain factory and museum).

If you have a car, try Hollókő (traditional village, folk costume) and Szécsény (a leaning church tower, mansion with a hunting museum, and the quintessential country town); Eger (Hungary's best

Baroque town, Lyceum, basilica, castle, wineries, and churches); Pécs (art galleries, Zsolnay Ceramics Museum Quarter, Baroque buildings, and Turkish remains); and Sopron (medieval town, museums, forests). Eger, Pécs, Sopron, and Sümeg are accessible by train from Budapest, but will take a little time.

The young will enjoy Szentendre outskirts (open-air museum); Visegrád (ruined palaces and castles, Danube views, summer bob—bobsleighs with wheels); Ipolytarnóc (23,000,000-year-old fossils and footprints); Szilvásvárad (Lipizzaner stud farm, carriage museum, waterfalls); Aggtelek (a vast cave system that extends into Slovakia—home to rare bat species), Hortobágy (horsemanship); Balatonfüred (bathing, boating, and Balaton shipping); and Tihany (views, abbey).

HEALTH

The state health service suffers from uneven standards of provision, and the morale of health staff, who are paid miserable wages, is poor. As a result, reports of bad treatment are legion in the domestic press. Yet, the feedback from tourists who are in need of emergency care is surprisingly good. Nonetheless, most long-term expats with corporations have private medical insurance. EU citizens are entitled to free medical care, and other foreigners to emergency care. The gratuities that Hungarians routinely slip to doctors for guaranteed proper treatment are not expected from foreign patients.

SECURITY

Budapest and Hungary in general are normally very safe, with the incidence of violent crime against the person very low. However, visitors should take sensible precautions: avoid leaving valuables in cars, and be wary of pickpockets in areas with crowds, such as railway stations, rush-hour travel on public transportation, and even Danube boat trips.

There is far more risk of scams than violence: men in particular should be especially careful of "accidentally meeting" attractive English-speaking girls in downtown Budapest who, naturally, are happy to be invited out for a drink or meal. In one particularly infamous incident a pair of Scandinavian men ended up exchanging—with an escort of restaurant "heavies"—US $7,500 for a dinner for four in a pleasant but ordinary restaurant. Some night club-discos also charge outrageous prices for drinks, and tourists who object are roughed up. As one Western diplomat recounted: "These bouncers are very brutal. We had one man beaten to pulp a week or so back."

While emphasizing that the vast majority of visits are trouble free, the US and UK embassies both have advice pages with tips on avoiding scams and other crime on their Web sites.

Do not be tempted to change money on the street (the once advantageous black market rate is long gone) and if given an offer, and subsequently approached by "police"—do not respond to requests to show them your money. They are almost certainly imposters on a scam.

Genuine police are normally helpful to tourists, but you may well need an interpreter to report a crime. An official ID (a passport or driver's license with a photograph) should be carried at all times. Among the offenses most commonly committed by foreigners in Hungary are driving under the influence of alcohol and other traffic offenses. Seek legal advice immediately if more than a small fine is at stake.

chapter eight

BUSINESS BRIEFING

THE ECONOMY

Anyone teleported into one of Budapest's modern office complexes, filled with besuited, smiling business folk, could be forgiven for thinking they were in a top-performing Western economy. Alas, many parts of provincial Hungary, and even areas of the capital, tell a different story. In other words, economic life varies widely across the country, with the capital, and the west–northwest generally, well in advance of other areas.

Some facts: Hungary ranks 109th among the countries of the world in territory, 91st in population, and 60th in GDP, the commonest measure of the size of an economy. In 2014, GDP per capita, at purchasing power parity, stood at almost US $25,000, or roughly two-thirds the average of the European Union.

So while in world terms Hungary is developed, with around 80 percent of the economy in private hands, in European terms it is still an emerging economy. The average wage in 2016 was around €850, or US $940, per month.

Nonetheless, despite commonly expressed nostalgic yearning for the Communist era, living standards for large swathes of the population are light-years ahead of how things were in 1990.

THE DRIVE TO EXPAND LOCAL BUSINESS

The successes achieved by foreign investors in Hungary, whether in terms of greenfield investments or of rejuvenating ailing domestic companies, have been something of a two-edged sword. Hungarians—from politicians cutting ceremonial ribbons to the formerly unemployed in the surrounding crowd—clap enthusiastically at news of a new foreign-owned factory or production hall being inaugurated. Yet these same Hungarians at other times will lament, if not resent, the fact that the business owner is non-Magyar.

To be sure, serious Hungarian companies are out there: at the head of the list is Mol, the oil and gas group with 2015 revenues of US $15 billion, which has exploration projects from the North Sea to Pakistan, service stations across the region, and complex refining operations in Croatia and Slovakia. Similarly, OTP Bank has busied itself with acquisitions, while drug maker Gedeon Richter has successful exports from North America to Russia.

Videoton is an outstanding example of a successful privately owned domestic company. An automotive components and household goods manufacturer that metamorphosed out of a Communist-era electronics company, it is Hungary's largest private manufacturer, with revenues of c. €500 million and almost 10,000 employees in Hungary and subsidiaries in Bulgaria, Germany, and Ukraine. Smaller, dynamic Masterplast is a child of the new age. Founded in 1997, it specializes in insulation materials and boasts turnover of €84 million, with subsidiaries in ten countries.

There are also many successful IT companies (see box page 155) among the thousands registered at the company courts. Yet, not enough are effective.

"There are some very successful, Hungarian-owned big companies, but small and medium-sized companies really don't play an important role in the economic performance. Most of these small, micro companies are only for family financing, to maintain the family budget and to buy some cars and so on. They do not develop significantly," says Éva Palócz, director of the Kopint-Tárki Institute, a Budapest-based economic think tank.

Why is this? The reasons are many and varied, but inadequate education plays a part, and within this, relatively poor linguistic skills. So, too, is the general business environment, which suffers from allegations of corruption and lack of transparency, and is continually subjected to tax and legal changes. The latter, critics say, are sometimes specifically designed to benefit politically favored companies over others.

Another problem area is the courts: trials can take years to reach a final verdict, and anyone in dispute with a politically well-connected person or institution can expect a very tough time indeed.

The OECD, in its May 2016 report on Hungary, noted: "Frequent changes in the regulatory framework undermine investment incentives . . . The effectiveness of the competition framework is reduced by exemptions to the application of competition policy."

In short, government action—cronyism and state-capture—undermines the government's very own declared policy of encouraging the growth and expansion of domestic companies.

THE BUSINESS ENVIRONMENT

"I've been in the situation hundreds of times with a Hungarian who throws his hands up in the air and says: 'This is impossible!' I say: 'OK, I understand. But what is the *kis kapu* [the "little gate," that is, the way round this]?' And he then smiles and starts explaining how it's done," says a senior partner from a "Big Four" professional services firm in Budapest. "It's the same as anywhere; you've got to get into the mindset. Things won't work the way you are used to."

The above quotation says a lot about Hungary and the business environment. Of course, this senior partner was not seeking an illicit or illegal way, but an acceptable solution that would usually not be obvious to the outsider. Such thinking was essential to survival in Hungary during Communism, and, despite the changes, it still persists—indeed, sometimes needs to persist in the light of fast-changing and often hastily prepared legislation.

One example of such persistence is the gray, that is, legal but untaxed, economy. There has been a long battle to ensure that waiters, hairdressers, and others such as the medical profession (yes, really) pay at least some tax on the tips they receive. Then there are the many self-employed—though employed in an economic sense, working for one "customer" on a regular basis—who have started a small company with their spouse and pay themselves a minimum wage.

The Orbán government has made positive moves in this area: it has required all retail outlets to link up online with the tax authority, thereby curbing unrecorded sales. It also introduced a flat rate of personal income tax of just 16 percent, which somewhat reduced the incentive to under-report earnings. Critics, however, say this fails to address the total wage costs, which include high social security payments. Moreover, the flat tax clearly most benefited the well-paid, while raising the VAT rate to 27 percent to help compensate for the loss of budget revenues disproportionately affected the low-paid.

This is not to say that government behavior has always been rational or honest. Accusations are easily made and difficult to prove. Indeed, according to the 2015 Transparency International Corruption Perceptions Index (CPI), Hungary received 51 points, compared to 54 points in 2014. (On the CPI, 0 points equals highly corrupt, and 100 equals squeaky clean.) This ranking puts Hungary just below Saudi Arabia, but marginally better than Kuwait in respondents' estimation of the pervasiveness of corruption.

BUSINESS RELATIONSHIPS
Some Hungarians in business still think mainly in terms of personal relationships—with their colleagues, their superiors, and their customers and suppliers. Historically, this had a lot to do with the Communist system, which left only personal relationships intact.

For you, the foreign businessperson, such thinking brings a need to identify a single person in a partner firm to whom you relate and with whom you do business. He or she will deal with the rest, where possible. If your link isn't there, don't expect anyone to stand in. Your file will patiently await his or her return, which will be annoying if you're in a hurry.

Such attitudes have been changing, certainly in foreign-owned and modern-thinking Hungarian companies, yet a 2015 study reveals change is slow. In total, 68 percent of Hungarian respondents were in agreement, or strongly in agreement, with the statement "It is important here to form friendships with colleagues and customers"—although this was down from 73 percent in a similar, 2009 study.

Intriguingly, while most expatriate and local managers in the region generally rate female managers highly, Hungarians are the exception. "Hungary was the country which, as in our 2009 survey, disputed this the most," says Klemens Wersonig, chief executive at Target International Executive Search, which co-sponsored the research.

HIERARCHY

That same survey reveals that firms in Hungary (and across the region) are typically hierarchical, with 64 percent of respondents disagreeing with the statement, "Hierarchies here tend to be informal."

If you are working with one of these more traditional companies, it means decision making takes time. You may have agreed to something with your partner, only to find the decision unexpectedly overruled higher up. Where talks are being conducted with a team of Hungarian negotiators, the ones who do the talking may be the ones who speak the best English, rather than the most senior. Even then, it's important to identify who is the boss, and show respect by making clear you are addressing that person, not the linguistic leader.

It's often the case that you discuss everything and seem to be reaching agreement, but no one in the room is qualified to clinch the deal. So it's extremely valuable to know something about the team beforehand. Job descriptions on business cards are a start, of course, but inquiries can be made of earlier contacts in the firm or secretarial staff while you're waiting. This is not classified information.

GOOD MANNERS

When you visit someone's office, shake hands all around, introduce yourself, and sit down only when invited. Be restrained in your body language. Take the opportunity to compliment your hosts on their premises, their furniture, the town, the district, the view. If you are offered some refreshment, accept it. This is the time to relax a little and build up the personal relations that mean so much to Hungarians. Don't show impatience if the meeting is interrupted. Hungarian executives must keep several balls in the air at once.

A visiting businesswomen will probably find a scarcity of women in positions of authority in Hungary. She may consider the courtesies of her Hungarian hosts to be old-fashioned, but they should be accepted with politeness and respect.

Hungarians may confuse Anglo-Saxon informality with insolence. Hierarchy again: if you are insufficiently polite, it may appear to the Hungarian that you're underestimating his or her status. If you should receive someone in your own office, stand up, apologize if you're on the telephone, offer a comfortable seat, and sit down with your guest away from the desk. Offer some token hospitality—coffee, say, or mineral water.

It's always worth remembering how reluctant Hungarians are to do business with someone they don't like. A pleasant, sympathetic approach is extremely valuable, because it breeds confidence in your potential partners. Condescension, on the other hand, doesn't work well at all, as many Western business advisers found when they were flown in after the collapse of Communism. Be charming and attentive, and avoid shows of irritation—if you want to do a deal, that is.

SERVICE WITH A SNORT

Having painted a picture of old-world courtesy in business offices, it has to be said that at a lower commercial level, for example in shops, many Hungarians are abrupt with their customers. Such sloppy service reflects low levels of staff training, pay, and status, and preconceived, simplistic ideas of how a deal should go: here it is, take it or leave it.

One key commercial concept lacking in many small and even medium-sized Hungarian firms is the repeat order. Where will the firm be by the time you need your next car, or insurance policy, or lakeside apartment let? The company is undercapitalized, and needs your money now. Buy, or stop wasting its time.

So what happens if you buy something that's faulty? Oddly enough, there aren't many problems if you have proof of purchase. Troubleshooting is something that many Hungarians seem to enjoy. The real trouble arrives when undercapitalized firms start giving ten-year maintenance guarantees—on a new apartment, for example.

PRESENTATIONS AND NEGOTIATIONS

Hungarians are used to speakers who begin an address with "I'll just say a few short words . . ." to be followed by a twenty-minute ramble, typically mumbled, *sans* microphone, into the ether. And if there is interpretation, the presenter is usually blissfully unaware of the difficulty the average interpreter has in handling the specialist language of subjects, which could include anything from gas transmission via project finance to agricultural fertilizers. And the mother of all disastrous delivery methods? Reading from a script, a guaranteed way of testing the soporific resistance levels of the most attentive audience. (Reading from the screen of a power point presentation is almost as bad.) Indeed, if there is one field of human activity in Hungary that is most impervious to the winds of change, it is making an interesting, effective presentation. Naturally, there are exceptions, chiefly among the under-thirty age group, but the Western visitor should take note and not replicate the problem.

When presenting, even if the audience all speak English, be aware that hearing, absorbing, and evaluating a line of thought in a foreign language takes more time for a non-native speaker. If using an interpreter, hold back and make sure the interpreter feels you appreciate them taking time to get the right meaning across, rather than rushing out inexact words.

Take time, and make eye contact wherever possible across your audience. If it is anything more than half a dozen people, use a microphone if available. Avoid references to cricket, baseball, or American football—they are hardly known in central Europe and will not be understood. Cracking jokes is a difficult area and best avoided, unless you check the idea first with a native you can trust who understands both you and the audience.

On the other hand, a well told, amusing, and relevant anecdote, perhaps involving the speaker's naivety on visiting the country, may be well received.

Hungarian audiences are typically passive—all the more so if they have not understood you correctly, and they are shy of speaking in English, perhaps afraid of making mistakes. Asking "Can you understand?" is usually a waste of time—very few individuals will be brave enough to say "no"—so it is the presenter's job to make sure they understand.

Prepare to make your key points from different angles, perhaps with an example: if feedback confirms your point is understood first time, you can drop the second approach.

When pitching a product, state your case clearly and positively, but do not exaggerate. If it's the best in the world, fine, but back this up with credible evidence. Be careful to avoid giving the impression that the USA or Western Europe has all the answers for "backward" central Europe—Hungarians are very proud of their technical prowess and innovation, and will find this offensive, even if they do not say so.

When negotiating, it's good to have a concession or two in hand, show an appreciation for the other side's difficulties, but make it clear, firmly but politely, when your limits are reached. If they don't want to pay for a quality product, then they won't get that quality for the price they are demanding.

CONTRACTS

Hungary is governed primarily by continental-style law, not Anglo-American case law (although in some areas of business, such as finance and real estate, certain Anglo-American practices and norms are quite strong). Traditionally, sellers, contractors, and providers in Hungary pay little attention to deadlines. Penalty clauses in a contract are often treated as if they themselves are up for repeated renegotiation. Let's forget the penalty clause for another couple of weeks and we'll have the work done by then, they suggest, hoping you don't have the energy to dismiss them and find someone else.

The heart of the matter lies in contractual relations. First, the spoken word doesn't constitute an undertaking of any kind in Hungarian business. At best, it means "I like the idea and I'll see how it goes." A contract in Hungary is not a contract until it's been negotiated, drawn up in due form, and signed and stamped before witnesses, best of all before a notary. Even then, if it turns out to be detrimental or inconvenient to one party, that party could ignore it.

Doing business successfully, after all, rests on considerations that go beyond a specific contract—honesty, trust, reputation, and the prospect of future business relations. Again, things are changing at better-run, modern-thinking companies, but Hungarian business is all too often thwarted by short-termism: cynical reliance on the fact that pursuing small claims through the courts is expensive and time-consuming.

CRONIES AND CREATIVITY

Faced with the remaining inherited shortcomings of the business environment, Hungarians have two lines of defense. One is cronyism. Whatever cronyism may be in other parts of the world, it's plain business sense here. Although foreigners in Hungary are short of relatives and old classmates, who make the best cronies of all, they too can start picking up friends and involving them in their business. This tendency has been reinforced in recent years based on political allegiances.

OUTSIDERS ON THE INSIDE— SOME CRITICAL QUOTES

"Hungarians can be very closed minded, hardly capable of accepting any other opinion. They often take professional suggestions too personally." *Twenty-four-year-old professional woman, hospitality sector.*

"There is a reluctance to resolve problems. Even the smallest issues are blown up and considered as show stoppers. Whenever there is a possibility not to change something they will take the opportunity." *Consultant, male, MBA.*

"Poor customer focus? I think every manager experiences it every day: when you have a problem with, say, an IT supplier. You call them, and the first reaction is always to throw the ball back. It's always your fault—you made a mistake because etc, etc." *Headhunter, male, twenty-five years experience in Hungary.*

From such quotes, along with the management study (referred to above) and discussions with numerous people involved with business in Hungary, it's clear there is much "old-style" thinking still present in business today.

People imbued with such concepts typically find it difficult to take on responsibility; they do not naturally take to teamwork or share information with colleagues and—perhaps the most commonly mentioned frailty—they take professional advice or suggestions as personal criticism.

And yet, this is the country of Ernő Rubik, inventor of the multicolored cube that fascinated the world in the 1980s. And as proved by the global success of companies like Graphisoft, Prezi, and Ustream (see page 155) there are Hungarians who can slot into any environment, create and run innovative teams, and take up challenges with Steve Jobs-like enthusiasm.

And it's not just in IT and "cool hi-tech industries" where Hungarians revel. Gergő Lencsés is manager of a GE-owned plant a few miles east of Budapest, a US $130 million investment that has been manufacturing heavy-duty gas turbine components since 2001. Now host to some 1,500 employees, the plant's products are exported globally.

"We're doing real world-class manufacturing, it's not just putting together three pieces of something and shipping it, Mr. Lencsés says, "We are improving productivity; we can ship units to Venezuela, and [still] be competitive."

HUNGARIAN HI-TECH SUCCESS STORIES

Hungarians are proud of their ingenuity, and there is invariably much stress on achievements by Magyar innovation in promotional trade material, not to mention pub talk. Nevertheless, Hungarian scientists, engineers, and medical researchers have contributed to many inventions and advances, and their successors in recent years have continued to fly the innovation flag.

Most particularly, by leveraging their expertise in mathematics and computer science, Hungary has produced a healthy crop of information technology (IT) successes. One pioneer of this trend is Gábor Bojár, a physicist, who in the early 1980s used a desk-top calculator to write a program for designing the cooling system for Hungary's Paks nuclear power station. He then developed this software into Archicad, today one of the most popular 3-D architectural design systems in the world.

Perhaps the most famous of the more recent start-ups is Prezi, a Web-based competitor to Powerpoint that allows users to create their own, dynamic presentations. Founded in 2009 by three Hungarians (two with a strong Swedish influence), Prezi boasted some 75 million users worldwide by mid-2016.

Ondrej Bartos, a Czech venture capitalist with investment across central and eastern Europe, says: "Hungarians, similarly to the number of Olympic medals per capita [they win], are fairly successful in IT."

chapter nine

COMMUNICATING

THE HUNGARIAN LANGUAGE

The Hungarian language belongs to the Finno-Ugric language family. It is spoken as a native language by 14.5 million people, of whom ten million live in Hungary. It is an isolated language, insofar as the main languages in all neighboring countries belong to other language families—Slavic (Slovak, Ukrainian, Serbian, Croatian, and Slovenian), Germanic (German), and Romance (Romanian)—so there is little structural similarity, even if some vocabulary is shared.

Hungarian vocabulary comes from several sources.

Although Hungarian contains only about 700 Finno-Ugric root elements, 60 percent of its vocabulary and an average of about 80 percent of any literary text are of Finno-Ugric origin.

In prehistoric times, there were strong Turkic and Iranic influences on Hungarian. Since the Hungarians settled in the Carpathian Basin at the end of the ninth century, many words and expressions have entered the language from Latin, Ottoman Turkish,

German, Greek, and Slavic languages—far more than is appreciated by the average Magyar. For example, four of the days of the week—*szerda*/Wednesday, *csütörtök*/Thursday, *péntek*/Friday and *szombat*/Saturday—are of Slavic origin (*szombat*, ultimately, is of Hebrew extraction). Even *hét* (week) derives from old Iranian.

More recently, significant numbers of French and English words have entered the language. Intriguingly, some English loan words have acquired different meanings: *szmoking* means a tuxedo, *winchester* a computer hard drive.

Among the commonest words of Hungarian origin in English are *biro* (ballpoint pen, from László Bíró, the name of its Hungarian-born inventor), and coach (from Kocs, a Hungarian cart-making village). Goulash, the typical soup-like stew of Hungary, gets its name from *gulyás*, a cowherd. Then there's hussar (*huszár*, itself of Slav origin), paprika (the Hungarian word for capsicum) and itsy-bitsy (*ici-pici*)—although the latter is disputed by academics.

Pronunciation
Though it may appear impossible on first hearing, an understandable pronunciation of Hungarian is certainly attainable for most English speakers. It just takes some effort. There are three general points.

The main stress always goes on the first syllable.

Short vowels (a, e, i, o, u) are distinct from long (á, é, í, ó, ú). There are also modified vowels, ö, ő, ü, and ű, pronounced as in *Löwe* in German and *tu* in French, short and long.

Long and short consonants are also clearly distinguished: tt is pronounced as in "set tea," not as in "pretty," nn as in "ten nuts," not as in "penny."

Here's a table of troublesome letters and letter combinations. The others are pronounced in a similar way to English.

Hungarian	Near English equivalent	
a	o	as in pot*
á	a	as in father
c	ts	as in pots
cs	ch	as in chop
dzs	j	as in jet
e	e	as in pet
é	ai	as in paid
g	g	as in got
gy	d	as in during
i	i	as in pit
í	ee	as in meet
j	y	as in yet
ly	y	as in yet
ny	n	as in new*
o	o	(with a round mouth)
ó	aw, oo	as in paw,* too
ö	a	as in about
ő	u	as in purple*
r	r	(trilled)
s	sh	as in shot
sz	s	as in spot
ty	t	as in tune*
u	u	as in put
ú	oo	as in boot
ü	ü	(as German, short)
ű	ü	(as German, long)
zs	s	as in pleasure

* = British pronunciation is nearer

THE MEDIA
The Press
Newspaper readership in Hungary has nosedived in the past two decades—generally put down to the combined effects of the Internet, a tendency to rely on television news, and poorer quality publications, which in turn is a consequence of dramatic downturns in advertising. State companies commonly shower pro-government media with advertising.

"Serious" national dailies still exist, just about, although the media market suffered the closure of the leading independent daily, *Népszabadság*, in 2016. That left *Magyar Nemzet*, *Népszava*, and *Magyar Hírlap*, plus newcomer, *Magyar Idők*, which was added in 2014. The latter, a government-supporting publication, was created after Prime Minister Orbán fell out with media mogul and former confidant Lajos Simicska. This row resulted in *Magyar Nemzet*, previously slavishly loyal to the government, turning hostile. Despite, or perhaps because of, this, its circulation tumbled to a mere 22,600 at the end of 2015, less than half of sales the end of 2010.

There are three national tabloids (one of them free) and two specialist dailies (business, sports), but people outside Budapest are more likely to read one of the local dailies in each of the nineteen counties.

There are a number of respected weeklies, including *hvg* (originally styled on the *Economist*), *168-Ora*, *Magyar Narancs*, and *Figyelő*—although in late 2016 the latter was bought by a new owner close to the government. *BBJ* (fortnightly, formerly the *Budapest Business Journal*) and *The Budapest Times* (weekly) are English publications, with the *Budapester Zeitung* as the latter's German-language equivalent.

All traditional print publications have their own Web sites, and there are a number of respected Internet news sites, led by index.hu, along with investigative sites such as 444.hu and direkt36. However, the journalism is often of mixed quality, with shoddy research, press releases published verbatim, fact mixed with opinion, and advertorial posing as independent journalism. This, as elsewhere, is in part due to cost and time pressures on editorial by the advent of the Internet.

However, the variety of independent news has been further undermined by a government decision to make news issued by MTI, the state news agency, available gratis, a move which has accelerated cuts in independent editorial staff across the industry.

Television and Radio
After a government-induced shake-up in 2011, electronic media are dominated by state broadcasting, all controlled through one umbrella holding company, Duna Media Service.

There are seven state-owned national television channels: M1 (all day news), M2 (children), M3 (retro), M4 (sports), M5 (education), Duna TV, and Duna World, but one more, M6, was due to be launched in late 2016. M1 has an English-language news program in the evening.

The two largest national commercial stations are RTL Klub and TV2. RTL Klub is owned by the RTL Group, and has been operating in Hungary since 1997. Its portfolio includes seven cable channels.

TV2, once seen as independent, has undergone a change in ownership and is now seen as loyal to the Fidesz government. The TV2 Group plans to have nine channels in its portfolio.

The other independent news channels are ATV and Hír TV, the latter having turned critical of the government in 2015 after the Orbán–Simicska split.

Cable TV is widely available, often with alternative packages that include English, French, Spanish, Chinese, Italian, Russian, and German stations. The biggest TV providers are UPC Magyarország and T-Home. Cable TV packages often include Internet and landline phones as well.

There are seven national public radio stations, complemented by half a dozen commercial stations (mostly controlled by ownership close to the government), and dozens of private local stations.

TELEPHONE AND INTERNET

The largely German-owned Magyar Telekom is the principal telephone provider in Hungary, serving around 75 percent of households. It is also the leading Internet and cell phone provider, with a little under 50 percent market share. However, there is competition from Norway's Telenor, the UK's Vodafone, and UPC. Romania's Digi is also set to join the fray.

Cell phone penetration has reached saturation point, with nearly 1.2 phones per man, woman, and child in the country. Mobile GSM 900/1,800 MHz services now provide 100 percent nationwide coverage, with 3G and 4G (LTE) networks just under 97 percent coverage. Service quality is outstanding.

All providers put out a bewildering variety of charging schemes, many including combined TV and Internet packages. Service information is usually available in English as well as Hungarian.

Mobile network companies use a variety of frequencies, especially for 4G (LTE) services, so US users should check with their chosen operator whether their existing handsets are suitable or not.

MAIL SERVICES

Post offices (marked Posta in a green and red livery) usually open at 8:00 or 9:00 a.m., but hours vary. Some close for lunch at some time between 12:00 noon and 2:00 p.m. Some close at 4:00 p.m., some as late as 7:00 p.m. Nearly all are closed on weekends. You can also buy stamps or postcards at a tobacconist or news vendor. There are mailboxes in front of post offices and elsewhere in the streets. Hungarians distrust these, and prefer to hand their mail over the counter.

The post office has a monopoly of letter and newspaper deliveries. The newspaper usually arrives, but the ostensibly daily deliveries of letters are erratic, and sometimes plain unreliable. Expatriates, for example, often report that books get "lost" in the post. (Tip: use a company address if possible.) Package and courier services are available.

Postcodes

Every address in Hungary has a four-figure postcode, the first digit denoting one of nine main postal areas. Budapest addresses begin with 1, for instance. Some other countries have four-figure postal codes, and for Hungary the prefix H– (for example, H–1028) can be used to avoid confusion. In many ways, the postcode is the most important part of the address to get right—a letter with just the name and postcode will often make it to the recipient.

CONCLUSION

Why do so many foreign visitors fall in love with Hungary? The first reason must be the Hungarians themselves, who are vivacious, amusing, inventive, and well-disposed toward foreigners. Those qualities make integration, even for a few days, a very pleasant and easy process for people of all ages. Hungarians have a sense of loyalty to their country and its assets that soon inspires newcomers too. It's also something worth cultivating. Hungarian books are worth reading, paintings worth viewing, and music worth hearing.

The climate is agreeable for nine months of the year, and there are ample opportunities for cultural, sporting, and outdoor activities. Some of the finest things in life—wining and dining—are good bargains. The pitfalls—shortcomings in infrastructure and service, visible social deprivation, slow bureaucracy— may be irritating, but they aren't usually dangerous.

The key to a rewarding stay is to make friends, for friendship is the stuff of Hungarian society. This book aims to help you make them. Not that it's difficult—an encounter with Hungary and its people is something that the visitor will never forget, and seldom regret.

Further Reading

Culture Smart! quizzed half a dozen people associated with both Hungary and international circles for their "best book" recommendation giving insight into the country and people—and this is what they suggested:

Relations, by Zsigmond Móricz. Budapest: Corvina Books, 1997.

Recommended by Péter Ákos Bod, professor of economics, Corvinus University, former governor of the National Bank of Hungary. Bod's reasons: "This is about the 1920s, Hungary, corruption and nepotism. But if you want to understand the present, it may be useful to read this wonderful piece of high literature."

Between the Woods and the Water, by Patrick Leigh Fermor. London: Penguin, 1988.

The choice of Col. Tim Manning, USAF, Chief, Office of Defense Cooperation, US Embassy Budapest, who says: "This is a true tale of adventure, romance, a vivid description of interbellum Hungary and deep insight to the history of the Magyars in the Carpathian basin."

My Happy Days in Hell, by György Faludy. London: Penguin Classics, 2010.

Selected by Rev. Frank Hegedus. "Even the title tells neatly of the contradictions of the Hungarian heart and spirit—joy in adversity, pluck in the face of tyranny. Faludy's improbable adventures abroad lead him back inevitably to the interior sojourn of prison life in his communist homeland," argues Frank, originally from the US Midwest, now chaplain of St. Margaret's Anglican Church, Budapest.

Under the Frog, by Tibor Fischer. New York: The New Press/ London: Polygon/Vintage, 1992.

Recommended by Dan Swartz, environmental activist and Marketing Assistant, Aggtelek National Park (Northeast Hungary). "A novel about a Hungarian basketball team traveling naked in a private train coach from game to game across Hungary during the 1956 Revolution," says Swartz, a native of Maine, USA, and long-time Hungary resident.

The Xenophobe's Guide to the Hungarians, Mátyás Sárközi & Miklós Vámos. London: Xenophobe's Guides, 1998.

Recommended by Priit Pallum, former ambassador of Estonia to Budapest: "This is the shortest book, reading-wise, to understanding the nation."

Zsuzsanna Szelényi, MP of the centrist Together party, champions György Dragomán's *The White King*, translated by Paul Olchváry, and published by Houghton Mifflin, Boston, in 2008.

"This heartbreaking novel offers an insight of the life of a child in totalitarianism, which reveals the typical past of many Hungarians and helps you understand the Eastern European experience, which still influences our personal behavior."

Other Recommended Books

Barber, Annabel, and Emma Roper-Evans. *Visible Cities. Budapest*. London/Budapest: Somerset Books, 2006.

Braham, Randolph. *The Politics of Genocide. The Holocaust in Hungary*. Detroit, MI: Wayne State UP, 2000.

Dent, Bob. *Budapest 1956, Locations of Drama*. Budapest: Európa Könyvkiadó, 2006.

Gáti, Charles. *Failed Illusions, Moscow, Washington, Budapest and the 1956 Hungarian Revolt*. Redwood City, CA: Stanford University Press, 2006.

Kertész, Imre. *Fatelessness*. New York/London: Vintage, 2004. Nobel Prize novel.

Lendvai, Paul. *Hungary: Between Democracy and Authoritarianism*. London: Hurst and Co, 2012.

Mautner, Zófia. *Budapest Bites. Spicy & Sweet Hungarian Home Cooking*. Budapest: Libri, 2015.

Molnár, Miklós. *A Concise History of Hungary*. Cambridge: CUP, 2001.

Phillips, Adrian, and Jo Scotchmer. *Hungary*. Chalfont St. Peter, Bucks: Bradt, 2010.

Smyth, Robert. *Hungarian Wine: A Tasting Trip to the New Old World*. London: Blue Guides Limited, 2015.

Rounds, Carol, and Erika Solyom. *Colloquial Hungarian*. New York and Abingdon, OX: Routledge, 2011.

Some Useful Web Sites

http://www.portfolio.hu/en/
http://www.hunglish.org/news/
www.hungarianspectrum.org
http://budapestbeacon.com/
http://bbj.hu/site/
http://hungarytoday.hu/
http://www.budapesttelegraph.com/
http://www.politics.hu/

culture smart! hungary

Index

Acknowledgments

Among the hundreds who assisted in this book, the authors would especially like to thank Áron Szőts, Zsófia László, Sándor Németh, Esther Ronay, Péter Pallai, Gábor Hegyi, Ervin Szűcs/staff at Webershandwick, Béla Király, Péter Radó, Györgyi Tóth, David Kirkby, Anita Gurney, Márton Dunai, Anikó Kardos, Gábor Bojár, Tibor Krebsz, Erika Kispéter, Judit Csernyánszky for their advice and comments.